# Four Fifty-Plus Fools Flit Fru France

# Also by Mike Newton

In Love with Japan (joint author Naoko Motohiro)

# Four Fifty-Plus Fools Flit Fru France

Four over-fifty year old men tour France, cycle over 900 miles from Biarritz to Caen, and pass through 16 towns twinned with British towns, raising money for five charities.

**Mike Newton**

iUniverse, Inc.
New York   Lincoln   Shanghai

# Four Fifty-Plus Fools
# Flit Fru France

**Four over-fifty year old men tour France, cycle over 900 miles from Biarritz to Caen, and pass through 16 towns twinned with British towns raising money for five charities.**

Copyright © 2006 by Michael E. Newton

All rights reserved. No part of this book may be used or reproduced by any means, graphic, electronic, or mechanical, including photocopying, recording, taping or by any information storage retrieval system without the written permission of the publisher except in the case of brief quotations embodied in critical articles and reviews.

iUniverse books may be ordered through booksellers or by contacting:

iUniverse
2021 Pine Lake Road, Suite 100
Lincoln, NE 68512
www.iuniverse.com
1-800-Authors (1-800-288-4677)

ISBN-13: 978-0-595-41760-5 (pbk)
ISBN-13: 978-0-595-86101-9 (ebk)
ISBN-10: 0-595-41760-4 (pbk)
ISBN-10: 0-595-86101-6 (ebk)

Printed in the United States of America

Text copyright 2005 by Mike Newton

All photographs taken by the author
Illustrations by Jeff & Pam King;
Christina & Alexandra Vamplew

Photographs illustrating the book
may be found on the website
http://www.1bm.me.uk/books/
and were all taken by Mike Newton

To Stephen and Stuart

I do not think there is any other quality so essential to success of any kind as the quality of perseverance. It overcomes almost everything, even nature.

John D. Rockefeller

Always bear in mind, that your own resolution to succeed is more important than any other thing.

Abraham Lincoln

The most rewarding things you do in life are often the ones that look like they cannot be done.

Arnold Palmer

# Contents

Acknowledgements . . . . . . . . . . . . . . . . . . . . . . . . . . . . .xiii
Farewell Messages . . . . . . . . . . . . . . . . . . . . . . . . . . . . . .xv
France showing the route . . . . . . . . . . . . . . . . . . . . . . . .xvii
GASBAGS . . . . . . . . . . . . . . . . . . . . . . . . . . . . . . . . . . . . .1
Biarritz . . . . . . . . . . . . . . . . . . . . . . . . . . . . . . . . . . . . . .12
The Pyrenees . . . . . . . . . . . . . . . . . . . . . . . . . . . . . . . . .32
Perigord, Quercy and Gascony . . . . . . . . . . . . . . . . . . . .58
The Massif Central . . . . . . . . . . . . . . . . . . . . . . . . . . . . .85
The Loire Valley . . . . . . . . . . . . . . . . . . . . . . . . . . . . . .109
Normandy . . . . . . . . . . . . . . . . . . . . . . . . . . . . . . . . . .161
Post-ride Activities . . . . . . . . . . . . . . . . . . . . . . . . . . . .182
Endpiece . . . . . . . . . . . . . . . . . . . . . . . . . . . . . . . . . . .195
Appendix . . . . . . . . . . . . . . . . . . . . . . . . . . . . . . . . . . .199
    A    Luggage and Equipment . . . . . . . . . . . . . . . . . .199
    B    Sponsorship . . . . . . . . . . . . . . . . . . . . . . . . . . .202
    C    Hotels . . . . . . . . . . . . . . . . . . . . . . . . . . . . . . .205
    D    Sponsorship Messages . . . . . . . . . . . . . . . . . . .206
    E    Possible Tour through the EU . . . . . . . . . . . . .208
    F    The Diary & Photographs . . . . . . . . . . . . . . . .209

# Acknowledgements

I would first like to thank the other three team members, Paul Greenhalgh, Ray Turner and John Harrison, who came on this biking trip across France and helped to make the experience so enjoyable. They, each by their actions, have provided good material for this record of the ride. I would especially like to thank Paul, who was committed to the ride from the start, and whose exuberance for both the ride and getting sponsorship matched mine—without Paul the ride would not have happened.

I would also like to thank all the members of the Great Ayton and Stokesley Biking and Guzzling Society (GASBAGS), with whom I have been on so many enjoyable bike rides; my partner Naoko for her support in checking my drafts and for her translation of the 'The Tour through Twinned Towns' website into Japanese; Jeff & Pam King, Christina & Alexandra Vamplew for producing excellent illustrations from my very rough drawings; Carol Morgan for twice including articles about our ride into the Great Ayton 'Stream' magazine; Bob Lappin for editing articles so that they would be in a format acceptable to the Darlington & Stockton Times; Stuart McFarlane for including us four times on his Radio Cleveland show; Tony Torelli of Torellisport for his philosophy of JIT (Just-in-Time) viz delivering the GASBAGS bike shirts just prior to the 2003 GASBAGS Xmas ride, and my extra two shirts just prior to this ride; Didier and Jocelyn for their wonderful hospitality in Ouzouer; Denis and Genevieve Brule in Lignieres for treating us like honoured guests; Dupont Teijin Films employees for helping my own efforts in raising sponsorship; all the other people who sponsored us on the ride; Jeff

& Pam King, 'Bushy' Ray & Bridget Vamplew for flying to Biarritz to wave us goodbye.

# Farewell Messages
## (From our GASBAGS Friends)

### When there were Two

Two tragic thick-skinned tossers
touring through tortuous twisting terrain
through Twin Towns towards the Tees together
tossing and turning,
totally traumatised in tight trousers
and twisted and torn testicles.

### When there were Four

Farewell to the four fifty plus fools as they fly and flit fru
France fiendishly frought but feeling fitter and fruitier.
Like four frisky ferrets, forsaking all farting and flatulence, the friends will be fed frequently with fresh food and full-bodied fine French wine.
As their feet flag and their flab fades, they will fink of the fortunate friends flukily frolicking in the fly n firkin.
May good fortune go with you—Forwarding wishes to you all
Flourish not flounder
Be focussed not fatigued and
Have full, not flat tyres

Love Zoe and Craig

# France showing the route

xvii

# GASBAGS

Ian and I had just arrived at the Black Horse in Swainby and the rest were some way back as they had stopped to look around the reservoir near Osmotherly. Ian bought me a pint and we sat down. "Thanks Ian. This must be our third pint by now," I said, "and we've only cycled twenty-five miles."

"You lot certainly enjoy a drink as much as you enjoy cycling," responded Ian. I've been in the CTC for four years and I've drunk more beer in four weeks with GASBAGS than I've drunk in all my time with the CTC."

"I think our GASBAGS name is well suited with it including the word 'Guzzling'," I laughed.

"How did GASBAGS start?" he asked.

"If you don't mind I will explain about my biking background before the rest arrive then they can get involved in explaining about GASBAGS."

Ian just supped his pint.

"I didn't take to biking until 1989 and by then I was forty. I had always been much more fascinated with any sport that included a ball. Between the ages of fifteen and twenty-six I had been in love with table tennis and dreamt of touring England (and the World) giving exhibitions and earning a living from being a ping-pong star."

"I really liked table-tennis as well when I was young but had no fantasies about being that good. Anyway biking was my main enjoyment."

"I played for the Boys Brigade team representing the local Baptist church as the team were entered in the UK championships, even though I was an atheist—I am now a humanist by the way. In order to be selected for the team I had to attend church a few times and then participate in a meeting of the Boys Brigade after the service. One day we were asked if we believed in God and everyone put up their hand, though some very slowly and reluctantly, except me—I held by my principles and gave my atheist view though I recognised it might have affected my team membership. Fortunately the lay preacher must have thought I could be saved and I retained my place. We went on to become the English champions but lost to a Scottish team in the UK final."

"Perhaps God recognised you were a fraud!" Ian laughed.

"At University I played for the University team and we reached the UAU finals with my flatmate ranked fourth in England, playing for our team. He was such a talented player that it taught me that I was never going to make a living out of table tennis when I found it difficult to even get a point from him."

"It must have great to practice with him though."

"It was but unfortunately we lost in the final as just beforehand our star player was diagnosed with having a twisted testicle and couldn't play."

"That's funny," Ian laughed. "So rather than playing with table tennis balls he had the doctors playing with his!"

I continued though Ian's eyes had begun to glaze over. "I also took to playing tennis and finally played for the school team but had no delusions of being a great tennis player. Squash became my main ball game when I had a young family as I enjoyed the thrash around, and the quick pint in the bar. One opponent, Rod Hardbattle smacked me right between the eyes with his racquet with his follow through, with blood rapidly filling the court."

"It sounds like his name reflects his game. I bet you missed your pint that day! You certainly like different sports."

"I do but I had given up most of them. At the age of thirty-nine I began to realise that I had more time to myself as my family was growing up, and I joined the local tennis club and restarted the Men's league team which had collapsed a few years earlier."

"So where does biking come in?"

"I was about to come to that. I had a bike but I found it rather boring to ride all the way to Stokesley from Great Ayton, a distance of 3 miles. It seemed pointless to ride on a bike when a car was so much faster."

Just then the rest arrived. "I was just telling Ian how I got into biking."

"Hope he has not been boring you too much," said Ray.

Ian was non-committal.

"I had just reached the point about how we began to go out on the bikes, Ray."

"I remember," Ray replied. "I was used to cycling vast distances and the only way I could get you on a bike was to stop at pubs every few miles."

"You're right," I guffawed, being affected by the beer. "I hadn't really liked cycling until then but the idea of mixing it with boozing seemed much more interesting. I was apprehensive that you would turn out to be too fit with all your fell running. I remember that you had very fit legs with nodules sticking out of your thighs like a Tour de France cyclist. You seemed to enjoy the beer though."

"I did. And the crisps."

"You always tied a knot in empty crisp packets—I could never understand why!"

"Better than smoking."

That's when you and Jeff got involved," I said to Bushy Ray, who had acquired his name due to his big bushy beard and had been listening.

"I used to really enjoy cycling when I was young but had given it up. However Mike and Ray's enthusiasm got me started again."

I turned back to Ian. "It was in 1990 that I had the idea that it would be good to cycle 100 miles, and proposed a route of

Great Ayton to Whitby to Scarborough to Helmsley to Stokesley and back to Great Ayton."

"I thought it was my idea," said Jeff, who had just turned round to get involved in our conversation.

"No—it was definitely mine," I responded. "I remember the day I proposed the ride very clearly. You three were enthusiastic though Jeff tried to change the route so that we went the other way round."

"You're right," Ray laughed. "Even then Jeff was trying to change the route. We all overruled him."

"I just like to look at options," Jeff responded pretending to be upset. "Some one has to play devil's advocate."

"But why is it always you," Bushy Ray chortled.

"I remember the ride well," I said. "We set off early one morning. The cycle to Whitby was very quick though all of us except you Ray," I said, "had to walk up the steep Birkbrow hill."

Jeff continued, "We stopped for breakfast in Whitby at what we nicknamed 'the greasy spoon' restaurant, and wolfed down bacon sandwiches."

"It was just outside Scarborough that disaster struck. I was about fifty yards behind you, Bushy Ray," I said, "when I saw a child run out on the road and you swerved and shot over your handlebars, and lay there not moving. You weren't wearing a helmet and I thought you had struck your head."

"I was even closer than you Mike. I jumped off my bike and ran over to him. He was not moving. I thought his breathing had stopped. I was about to give him mouth-to mouth resuscitation," said Jeff. "I was very concerned. I'd never practised it before on a person with a big bushy beard. Stupid thoughts went through my mind—would I get hairs between my teeth?"

"I was in a dilemma. I had been videoing the ride, but I thought it was inappropriate to film Bushy Ray's last moments—his wife, Bridget, might have wondered why I was not doing something more helpful," I laughed. "I also saw your head move towards Ray's—I thought you were going to kiss him! I thought Ray must have said 'Kiss me Hardy' in his dying breath."

"I hadn't realised that Bridget was Bushy Ray's wife—you are all so friendly," Ian said.

"I was so glad when you moved and you began to groan—at least you were alive," Jeff said.

"I thought thank god! We wouldn't have to inform your wife that you had gone to the cyclist heaven in the sky," I laughed.

"I remember feeling rather painful and limping as I got back on my feet. I looked about to check my bike and saw you holding it, Ray," said Bushy Ray.

"Those two were looking after you so I rescued your bike. Cars might have driven over it—it was fortunate that it was undamaged except for a slight buckle of the front wheel."

"You've always been more a bike person than a people person," Jeff laughed. "But seriously it was good that you sorted out the bike."

"We arrived in Scarborough after fifty miles," I continued.

"I was still hurting and hobbled round whilst our biking guru, messed around with my buckled wheel," said Bushy Ray.

"It was after we resumed that I felt a pain developing in my right knee," I said. "I thought I would have to bow out of the ride but you lot gave me lots of encouragement and I kept on—I was astounded that the pain totally disappeared the next day!"

"Just before Helmsley the rain came down fast and we got a soaking as none of us had brought weatherproofs. I stupidly believed the forecast of dry weather—I'm normally quite good with the weather," Ray said. "We finally reached Clay Bank, above Great Broughton, just after six after cycling over 100 miles."

"So how did this lead to GASBAGS?" Ian asked looking slightly exasperated.

"A bond had been formed between us—there's nothing like a near death for that," I said, "and our cycling trips became regular and other men became interested and joined our group. We named ourselves GASBAGS, the 'Great Ayton and Stokesley Biking and Guzzling Society'. The name reflected our group's philosophy well, as the biking was incidental compared to the chattering or gasbagging on route and drinking and guzzling in the pubs. I remember one short cycle ride when we reached a pub at nine in the evening and left to cycle home one hour later after consuming four pints of beer—my bike found it difficult to keep going straight and suddenly shot off onto the pavement then resumed its travel back on the road. I wondered if there was an offence 'Drunk and disorderly behaviour on a bike'." I chuckled.

I continued, "Each year we planned a major ride of over 100 miles, including cycling round the Scottish Islands a few times, and three Coast-to-Coast trips. The new Millennium arrived and women now joined the group."

"You mean the wives and girlfriends," Zoe interrupted. "Some of us women are as fast at biking and able to consume just as much ale."

"You introduced us to that great sport of dancing on pub tables when totally inebriated," I laughed.

"You're only thirty-three now Zoe. Some of us more mature women aren't as fast as you," Bridget stated.

"The introduction of women, Ian, led to one man refusing to go out anymore if women took part," Jeff said.

"A right MCP," said Pam.

"Are you two husband and wife?" Ian asked. "You appear to work in tandem—excuse the pun."

"We are," Pam replied then giggled, "but sometimes I wish I could recycle him."

"In the same year as the women joined I built the GASBAGS web site, which recorded all our achievements and cemented my self-appointed position of GASBAGS chairman as no one else could change the web site," I guffawed, by now even more affected by the beer.

"We keep proposing other people as chairman," Zoe said. "I think there should be a woman chairman soon."

"So when did you get the bike shirts? They make you look like a real cycling club," Ian asked.

"For many years we had discussed designing and buying club shirts with GASBAGS stamped all over them but nothing had materialised," I said. "Then one day in early 2003 I walked into the Great Ayton biking shop Biketraks and saw shirts which they had had designed with 'Biketraks' and their web-site address all over them. I was smitten and became determined that GASBAGS shirts would be produced. I raised this issue at our regular Thursday night pub get-togethers, which were a weekly event whether we were biking or not."

"I enjoyed those winter weeks that we spent arguing over the layout of the shirts. First time I have seen you get angry Mike," Jeff said.

"I did get a bit exasperated, I agree," I continued. "We obtained standard templates from Torelli Sports, with lots of colour choices and we could choose the text and font style. Anyone watching would have thought we were at war as Jeff shouted to get different choices of colour."

"That's when I said, "We must look like a team and all have the same colour. I won't buy one if they are different"," Zoe laughed.

"I gave in at that point," Jeff chuckled. "I realised I was not going to get my way against you, Zoe."

"The fighting didn't stop then," I continued. "I was keen to include the words 'Great Ayton and Stokesley Biking and Guzzling Society' on the front and back of the shirts as I felt people reading our shirts would understand that we were not serious bikers whilst you Bushy Ray wanted just 'GAS-BAGS' to be shown so people could guess what it meant."

"I still think I was right," said Bushy Ray. "Anyway I lost that one."

"You did. I had to hold a secret ballot to quell your rebelliousness. I felt like a real politician as I trudged round everyone secretly to get their support."

"I didn't know about that," Bushy Ray responded angrily. "I think we should have a rerun."

"Don't be silly. We're wearing the shirts."

"We could ink out all the 'Great Ayton and Stokesley Biking and Guzzling Society' words on the twenty-eight shirts. I would do it."

"You see what I'm dealing with, Ian!" I said. "Life as chairman is not as easy as it seems."

"We have to thank you, Mike," Jeff said," for getting the shirts in time for our annual Christmas Eve ride."

"We almost didn't," I replied. "I pestered the supplier, Tony Torelli, again and again He phoned up straight after he arrived home from a night drive back from Belgium where the shirts were made. I jumped in the car that same day, December 23rd, and drove to Oldham. I returned post haste and handed out the shirts that evening."

"That was the best Christmas ride ever because of the shirts," Pam said. "There must have been twenty-two of us in our new shirts crammed into your kitchen drinking punch and eating mince pies."

"It was excellent," I responded. "The exuberance was immense, helped by the alcohol. I remember you, Bushy Ray, were still muttering, "I don't like the words 'Great Ayton and Stokesley Biking and Guzzling Society' on the shirts." I told you that you could be club president to keep you quiet."

"I really enjoyed the ride to the Blackwell Ox pub in Carlton," said Bridget. "I was near the back as we cycled through the Ayton main street and could see all the shirts in front of me. There were people shouting 'Come on GAS-BAGS'. I felt proud."

"I felt the same," I responded. "At last I felt we were a real club!"

"That took some explanation," laughed Ian. "I will tell the tale to my wife whenever she can't sleep."

"You deserve another pint, Ian," I responded.

"So what about this biking trip across France that you cycled last year—over 900 miles. I've cycled 200 kilometres in a day and would love to do a long ride some day. Whose idea was that?" Ian asked.

"This could be a very long explanation," warned Jeff chuckling.

"I have to admit it was my idea," I replied. "I began to think of holidays in the New Year after our bike shirts arrived. I now had a Japanese partner, Naoko, who, I realised, could only spend part of her time in England as she still had daughters at University in Japan. I thought a long biking expedition might pass the time when she was away. However, the thoughts of Lands End to John O'Groats gave me a feeling of wetness, cold, and congestion."

"I look forward to meeting Naoko," Ian said.

I continued, "I had recently half read a book about a woman who had biked across Spain by herself—half read as the book was left in a hotel by mistake. The half I did read gave me that thrill of cycling on an unknown route in a foreign hot country, where I would come back bronzed, muscular and, hopefully, some of my bulk might have disappeared in sweat."

"No doubt you sweat a lot," Bridget said. "So did you learn whether she completed her ride or was knocked down and killed?"

"Don't be so silly Bridget," responded Bushy Ray her husband. "She wrote the book so she must be still alive."

"She had hardly ridden a bike before and had the nerve to go on such an adventure by herself," I said. "I thought if she could do it then so could I. I looked at my map of Europe and decided on a route starting in the south of France and coming north."

"I remember you mentioning it at one of our Thursday night meetings, Mike," said Jeff. "I was going to volunteer until I glanced at Pam. I could tell she wanted me to keep quiet. At any rate I would have asked you to change the direction—I fancied ending up in Biarritz."

"That's when Paul spouted up that he would like to do it as he had been thinking of a trip like this for some time," I said.

"Who is this Paul?" Ian asked. "I've never met him yet."

"It's very strange," said Ray. "Ever since we returned from the French tour he has hardly been seen."

"So did you go on the ride?" asked Ian.

"Yes, but I was not in at the start of the planning. I was womanless at that point and was unclear on my future plans," responded Ray.

I continued, "It is odd, I agree. I think he is sorting out his garden this year. I initially thought his wife would firmly stop Paul from going away last year for the long period that this ride would require but no, she was enthusiastic for him to go."

"You'll enjoy meeting Paul," Bushy Ray said. "He's a fairly recent GASBAGS acquisition, and came on his first major ride in 2001. He fitted the GASBAGS standard profile well, was almost fifty and slightly portly, and enjoyed a good drink. He originates from Birmingham and still has a Brummie accent—but we still allowed him to join!"

"I never really discussed his biking experience in depth until we were actually going across France," I said. "I hadn't realised that biking had been his major sport all his life and he had ridden endless 100 miles rides. I regretted not having this knowledge when we planned the route."

"He's much fitter than he looks," Ray said. "He has the perseverance and ability to lose weight. He lost a few stone over the six months before the ride started. He has run in many half marathons including fourteen consecutive Great North Runs, with his last one being in 1999, and the London Marathon in 1997. Unfortunately he damaged his knee on a New Years Day run in 2000, and any thoughts of competing in a second London Marathon were dropped."

"He's into damaging himself," I said. "On our 2003 GAS-BAGS Annual ride around Dumfries and Galloway Paul fell off his bike. I watched Paul come down a hill and decide at the last moment to turn right but forgot to inform his bike which decided to go straight on. He did a wonderful flying rolling dive and I asked him to repeat it so I could capture him on my camcorder. He was like an Italian football star. Any Italian football club would have signed him up if they had seen him."

"I missed his accident," said Jeff, "But I saw him get up off the rough stones. I was surprised that he was not cut but he did suffer a broken bone in his elbow so that was the end of his ride. Three weeks later he was also diagnosed with having a fracture in his pelvis."

"He was lucky to suffer no permanent damage," Ian said. "Quite an achievement to cycle 900 miles after an accident like that."

"So that's how Paul acquired his new officer position in GASBAGS. He became 'The Rolling and Diving Advisor'," I guffawed. "I will now tell you the full tale of our cycle ride across France."

# Biarritz

## Wednesday August 18th

We arrived at Stansted Airport at seven in the morning and as yet we had not been forced to feel a bike seat, or go up hills. As we had driven down from Great Ayton we passed through torrential rain, something we hoped we wouldn't see in France. We ate our last English breakfast at the airport.

"It seems a long time since you and I had started to plan this bike ride," remarked Paul.

"You're right, Paul. It goes right back to January," I replied.

Paul laughed. "I enjoyed meeting every Monday night, with the beer we drank to stimulate our little grey cells."

"It suited me as my Japanese girlfriend, Naoko, was in Japan," I said. "We had quite a brainstorming session, I remember. We listed all the activities involved in the ride. We came up with the route, date, number of days, travel to Biarritz, travel back from Caen, accommodation, bike maintenance, bike packing, baggage required including clothes, insurance, advice and contacts."

"I'm glad I was not involved at that stage," said Ray. "It sounds much too detailed to me."

"I was worried initially about how much it would cost," said Paul. "Our rough estimate for twenty days came to £1,800 each. I thought it was quite high initially, but then I thought it would cost even more just to lie on a beach."

"I wonder if our cost breakdown will turn out to be correct. We guessed at £25 per night to stay in a hotel for twenty nights, £300 to travel to the start and from the destination of the ride, £50 per day for breakfast, lunch, dinner and refreshments," I said.

"I asked Paul if I could join you two in June, I remember," said Ray. "I had had no luck on the lady front and had plenty of spare holiday."

"When Paul told me that you wanted to join us, Ray, I was apprehensive about you coming," I said. "I may have known you since I moved to Great Ayton nineteen years go, but I was worried about you being much faster than me. I imagined seeing Paul's and your backsides disappearing into the horizon. I was also apprehensive about a three-some as it would be difficult to book accommodation."

"Paul told me that I would have to pay the full amount for double rooms. That prompted me to ask you, John," said Ray.

"I'm glad you did," said John.

"I was now apprehensive when Ray said he had asked a John Harrison as I was concerned about not having met you, John," responded Paul. "Especially when you weren't a member of GASBAGS! However, when Ray said he went on an off-road bike ride with you every Wednesday I felt better."

Ray, who works for the Ordnance Survey and is our expert on route navigation, remarked, "The foothills of the Pyrenees are much worse than they sound and perhaps more like ankle-hills than foothills."

I responded, "Shut up Ray, I prefer not to know."

I knew Ray enjoyed going up hills but this was not something I wanted to hear. I have always been slow going up hills, as I did not like the painful burning sensation in my thighs caused by lactic acid production.

John declared, "I love French breakfasts with the croissants, baguettes and cheese."

"But after two weeks I will be ready for a good fry-up," remarked Ray, letting out a burp.

I came in with, "I wonder how many mayors we will meet?"

"Probably none," John spouted.

"Don't forget you promised to wear a GASBAGS shirt if we do," Paul exclaimed.

"Huh," was John's response.

I declared, "Perhaps there will be crowds to greet us in the twinned towns. We certainly sent out enough letters and emails to the mayors, twinning associations, and cycling clubs. We should thank Paul for all his efforts."

"Thanks Mike. I was concerned though about the automatic French translations, like Reading being translated to Livre, and Goring being translated to Encorner. They might have been insulted," responded Paul.

"At least we tried. Well we have now been pledged over £2,000—not bad even before the ride has started," I declared.

John responded, "There will be no crowds—you delude yourself. How many twinned towns will we be passing through?"

"Sixteen in total now. I am fairly confident we will meet at least one mayor—at Ouzouer twinned with Great Ayton. I have met him before. He does tend to switch wives though so I doubt I will know his wife," Paul laughed.

"The website that you built, Mike, looks great with the map of France and the three legs in English, French and Japanese," Paul stated.

"Thanks Paul. You and I are like a self congratulatory society," I responded.

Ray said, "But very few entered their sponsorship on the site—we had to do most of it."

"But you didn't even tell anyone the site address so not surprising. I had quite a few enter directly once I kicked them hard enough," I responded.

Paul declared, "I still expect to raise at least £500 from a bunch of solicitor friends. Naoko did well to translate into Japanese—though I can't understand a word of it. It is a shame that there have been no Japanese entries."

Ray joked, "How do we know she has not totally changed our write-ups—we might be figures of fun in Japan right now!"

"I still want to know who is Paul Le Velo, our only sponsorship entry on the French leg. Admit it was you Paul! Paul Le Velo means Paul The Bike—you! I liked the message he left about it being just mad dogs and Englishmen that cycle in the mid-day sun," I said laughing.

"He is a friend of my Ouzouer friend's Didier and Jocelyne," Paul responded with a straight face.

I said, "Yes but you hadn't been able to contact them by the time Paul the Bike's sponsorship went on the site so how did he know the web address? This sounds like your doing."

"Not me," said Paul grinning.

Paul asked, probably trying to change the subject, "How much sponsorship have you entered on the website John?"

John decided to ignore this remark as we all knew that he had made no entries on the website. At this point Ray farted and we decided to leave the restaurant fast.

Ray is renowned for farting and could easily clear a restaurant. Just before we left England our young GASBAGS friend Zoe, just 31, gave the GASBAGS members on this ride dog tags to wear in case we got lost. Ray bought necklace loops for them—he was very proud of his and wanted to show everyone. It was inscribed 'Ray—Le Pong' for obvious reasons. Paul's was inscribed 'Paul Le Streak' for his speed bursts or his weight loss acquired during his training; mine was inscribed 'Mike Le Laptop' as I was prepared to carry my laptop across France. On the back of each was inscribed 'Tour de France'. Perhaps our tour was not as far as the real Tour de France but it was far enough for us old men.

We couldn't pre-book seats on RyanAir so I dived to get the front seat which had ample room to fit my two metre frame. I always had a dread of flying long distances since on one return flight from Japan to England several years ago I had been forced to fly economy class, as all the business class seats were full. My knees were jammed into the seat in front and the occupant objected vehemently so I politely informed him that my knees were attached to my body.

Paul, Ray and John were in the other front seats. The hostesses were hovering around in front of us and Paul's roving eye soon located the most attractive one. He was smitten and asked her name—Julia. He now became convinced that she was glancing at him (perhaps he had a piece of English breakfast stuck in his beard) but I think she must have had a squint as I thought she was eyeing me up.

I was surprised that Paul was still so sprightly as we had been up since two in the morning and he had informed me just before we arrived at the airport that he had had little sleep as he had been finishing off reports for work and packing his panniers in a mad last minute rush. If I had known I would at least have shared the five-hour drive—I felt lucky to be alive!

As the plane came into land at Biarritz we could see the houses with their bright red roofs and white or cream painted walls. The greenery looked very lush and the river was swollen, not too surprising as last week there was three inches of rain in a day. A wall of heat hit us as we walked off the plane just after one, fortunately 29 DegC not the 40 DegC, as in August 2003, that we had been dreading

The bikes re-appeared in their huge cardboard (six foot by four foot by eighteen inch) boxes. When we had booked with RyanAir we had been told that the bikes had to be packed in standard bike boxes and we had been able to obtain these from the local biking shop BikeTraks. We had all packed them in to the boxes over the previous weekend, removing the wheels, seats and pedals, and turning the handlebars round. Ray had even packed one of his back panniers in the box. We had Jeff to thank for providing plenty of bubble-wrap, which he had obtained from a rubbish dump.

We ripped them open and each of us hurried to rebuild our bike first without admitting it was a race. The sweat began to flow as we put back the front wheel, the seat, the pedals etc. I rode mine round the airport arrival area and became very concerned as the whole thing was shaking. I couldn't imagine cycling like this for 900 miles. However I let down the handlebars and the bike became more stable, but still a very different feel with the heavy panniers on the rear and the handlebar bag.

We now had the problem of getting rid of the boxes, a problem we had thought of but we had not come up with a solution to. We asked a French airport baggage woman if we could leave them neatly stashed in the airport baggage collection area but "non, non, non" was the answer.

Paul went to look outside, and soon re-appeared, he said, "I have found a bin in the car park."

He and I carried the boxes out.

I stated, "A tiny bin—they won't fit in that."

Paul responded, "We will stash them next to it—one on top of the other."

We laid the four enormous boxes by the side of the bin. As we hurried away I realised we could be traced as our names and addresses were on the boxes. I shouted to Paul, "Paul, we must remove the labels."

He turned round and we both rushed to tear off the labelled parts of the boxes and stuffed them in the bin. He remarked, "It may not help since the airport can contact the airline to check who flew out with the bikes from Stansted."

"That would be a real challenge to Interpol," I retorted.

"Perhaps the boxes will be waiting on our front-lawns when we arrive home!" Paul said laughing.

At that moment I saw what looked like an airport guard walking our way. We ran back into the airport lounge. I shouted to Ray and John, "Get on your bikes quick, we need to make a quick exit."

We biked rapidly away from the airport and immediately took a wrong turn even though Paul had thought to print the route off an Internet site. John remarked in a snide voice, "Who has planned this trip?"

Paul and I looked at each other with concern, each surprised to hear this remark from the last person to join up on the trip. We turned the map around a few times and finally headed off in the direction of the Tulip Hotel.

Paul and I had previously booked the Tulip Inn in Biarritz after Jeff had booked in our fan club (Jeff & Pam, Ray & Bridget) at a price of £24 per night each. We thought this price was very low for staying in a top resort like Biarritz, and gave us confidence that the cost of accommodation would be less than we initially believed it would be.

I had informed my GASBAGS friends some weeks before that I intended to take my laptop PC to write a diary, which brought hoots of laughter. They all thought I would have difficulty taking my bulk up hills and that the extra weight would be too much but I was confident that the impact upon my slow uphill pace would be negligible. Now I had to get it linked through to the Internet so I could update the website I had built for the ride.

The website was the centrepiece of the publicity. It contained a French Map with each twinned town marked on it and a line showing the route. Hotspots against the twinned towns enabled links through to detailed information about the towns and the English Twinned towns. Paul and I had then spent hours and hours on the Internet extracting information to add to the website about these towns, wondering if anyone would ever read the descriptions of the different towns!

I noticed in the hotel room that the phone connections were different to the English ones and determined to find the right connector to attach the PC. We changed and came down to explore Biarritz. "It's starting to bloody rain. I thought we left rain behind in England," Paul said despairingly.

"At least it's warm rain," I responded.

I called in at a French Telecom shop, tried my "Bonjour" and switched to English. Was saying "Bonjour" enough to show them I had tried and to placate the French pride? Fortunately the shop manager spoke reasonable English, and explained that buying a pay-as-you-go SIMM card would not allow data transmittal so I would not be able to download to the website through a mobile phone. My only possible way to access the Internet now seemed to be through the hotel phone connection points. I asked about buying a phone connector with a an RJ11 connector socket and he gave me directions to a shop, go left, go right, go up to the lights, go…by this time I was lost so I gave up and thought I would buy one once I reached Pau.

We stopped at the first café with outdoor seats and tried the beer. "That's really refreshing after the plane flight," stated John.

"I agree," responded Ray, "but I will be gagging for a pint of British real beer very soon. This is the normal tasteless gassy lager."

"You can't beat the beers sold in Yorkshire," Paul affirmed, "with the likes of Black Sheep and Theakstons."

The roads were packed with cars and there were crowds of people rushing past though faint drizzle was still in the air. We strolled down through the main square and onto the beach. "This beach reminds me of Blackpool, I laughed. "A few people will sunbathe whatever the weather."

"They're hoping the sun's going to come out," responded Paul.

"For years I have heard of the wonderful resort of Biarritz and now I am here I am wondering when I will see the wonderful parts," I declared.

We decided that we would like to eat but nowhere seemed to want to serve food till after seven, even though the pavement restaurants were full of people. We wandered back to the main square, sat down in a bar and looked down towards the sea with six storey stone buildings on either side, and an open-air domed concert platform between us and the sea. The rain subsided, a band began to play Spanish music and a group of women dressed in bright orange dresses began Flamenco dancing on the platform. More and more people were strolling about in the evening heat, and I began to feel the enchanting atmosphere of Biarritz.

Loud church bells began to sound, competing with the Spanish music. "I have never been a fan of loud church bells on a Sunday morning—what if the Queen song 'Bohemian Rhapsody' was played loudly instead—I bet there would be a few complaints," I declared.

"We could suggest to our local church that they should start a new trend of blasting out music across the village to suit the mood. They could play 'Bang-a-Boomerang' by Abba when they want the population to feel joyful," Paul responded.

"Or 'Yesterday' by the Beatles when they want a mood of inward reflection, or 'Satisfaction' by the Rolling Stones when they want to help conception," Ray laughed.

"Did you play 'Satisfaction' to help with conception Ray?" John asked.

"It certainly sets a good fast pace," Ray retorted.

"These bells make me think about the Shinto religion in Japan," I declared. "I visited many Shinto shrines when I went to Japan last March and they all had a large bell outside which you rang to wake the God inside the shrine."

"That seems to be an eminently more sensible idea than these churches that ring bells to try to attract attention to their existence," Paul asserted.

We chose a restaurant in the square and were served by a waitress with black hair, brown legs and a Brigitte Bardot pout (when she was younger—she is seventy this year). Paul was smitten for the second time in the day and asked her name: Muriel (I had noticed that Paul was very fast at asking attractive young ladies their name). He was particularly attracted by the fine bone structure of her face, and by her poise as she walked about the restaurant—his eyes followed her every movement. We each had fish soup followed by duck on sticks.

After eating we strolled through the square and along the seawall and saw the vast expanse of yellow sandy beaches. The streets were packed with people, many in shorts, with it being easy to tell the newly arrived British by their lily-white legs. We searched for our fan club (Jeff & Pam, Ray & Bridget) that had specially chosen to go to Biarritz to wave goodbye to us, though recently they had all seemed more intent to use the opportunity to have a holiday.

Our meeting resulted in lots of hugging as if we had met long lost friends when we had only seen them two days before. They had just visited Lourdes but no miracle seemed to have happened to them (even though Jeff brought a plastic bottle replica of the Virgin Mary to fill with "holy" water from the array of 'holy' taps—her head could be unscrewed to drink!).

I said to Jeff, "No miracle happened to you and Ray—you are still both bald and ugly."

"At least we have a woman who is not 6000 miles away", Bushy Ray retorted.

"Pam and Bridget, you two do look particularly alluring today in your shorts and brown legs that go all the way up to your backsides," stated Paul, ever the ladies man.

"You shouldn't be looking Paul—what would Liz say," giggled Pam.

Jeff remarked to John, "You must be the smallest ever GASBAG."

John frowned and replied, "I AM not a GASBAG!"

Jeff is not known for his tact or diplomacy—his GASBAGS post of 'Diplomatic Adviser' always produced laughter when mentioned. I wondered if John would still wear my spare GASBAGS shirt when we met all the mayors as he had promised.

"What's the background to Lourdes?" asked Ray.

"I read up about it", replied Bushy Ray, "It owes its celebrity to visions of the Virgin experienced by a little fourteen year-old girl, Bernadette Soubirous, in 1858."

I remarked, "These days we would assume she was on drugs and she would get a clip round the ear—that's of course if clipping round the ear is still politically acceptable."

Bushy Ray continued, "Four million people annually visit the Grotte Massabielle, the cave where the visions occurred, and room on rue de Petits-Fosses where Bernadette's family lived, in search of a miracle cure for disability or disease."

"I heard that if one is not led there by faith, Lourdes is best avoided or left to those who really need it—and after going there I can see why," Pam remarked, never keen upon crowds.

"Well I am very sceptical about any kind of miracle except when Boro beat Manchester United," I declared.

I must admit that I thought about religion a lot when I was in my teens and by my late teens was firmly in the atheist camp, which could rule me out for being an American President. I have now switched to saying I am a humanist as I firmly believe that the only intelligent impact on the world is by humans. I am sure if all humans believed this then there would be fewer wars in the world. Enough of my religious views!

Our new group of eight now took the opportunity to again consume more alcohol and we chose an outdoor cafe, staring at the wonderful vast blue sea and enormous waves as the darkness came down.

"How about staying here for three weeks. We could send back made-up stories of our biking exploits," Ray declared.

"We might meet more mayors that way," John laughed.

"It's a shame we didn't book to stay a few more nights," I responded.

"I'm glad I don't have to cock my leg over a bike for the next three weeks," Bushy Ray declared.

"You probably can't cock your leg over anything these days—you aren't far off sixty," I retorted.

"Don't be so sure," Bridget smiled sweetly.

Jeff stated, "Biarritz is a wonderful place. I have been wanting to come here since I was seventeen…almost forty years ago."

Jeff thought he could understand French, checked the drinks menu and said, "Trust me," and ordered what he thought was a special cheap brew of beer, Biere Panache. It turned out to be beer shandy much to our amusement and Jeff's chagrin.

## Thursday August 19th

I came down to breakfast to find John and Ray already there. The food available was very impressive: apple puree; creamy yoghurt; almond cake; etc, and more than the expected French standard breakfast of coffee, croissants and cheese.

After breakfast I went to check my bike as I had been rather concerned about its 'feel' yesterday but now with no panniers it seemed to be fine.

We all set off and strolled down to the sea and made our way through thousands of bodies that were absorbing the morning sun. The waves were dashing in with majestic white froth.

I remarked, "Did you see the few topless women—some very slim and attractive ones and well endowed."

"But some were like old whales—they would look more enticing with their clothes on," observed Ray.

I laid out my Micro-fibre Giant trek towel on the few square metres available. I said to Ray, "This towel you recommended me to buy was very expensive at £28. I hope I use it more than just on this beach."

"They are worth the price as they are six times lighter, take up an eighth of the packing space, and dry four times faster than a standard beach towel," Ray said as if quoting from a sales brochure.

"I also bought a little one to wipe off my immense sweat." I had no doubt I required them as standard towels would have taken up too much room.

I quickly changed and shouted to Pam and Bridget, "Are you two going in topless?"

"Go on," urged on Jeff.

"No way with you lot staring at me," responded Pam indignantly.

I ran down to join the crowds in the ankle-deep sea being held back by lifeguards and wondered why until I tried to paddle out and felt the strong undercurrents. Ray performed his normal entry into any water by doing a handstand then falling onto his back with a big splash. We lay on the beach for a time.

Paul remarked, "Best to lie low and hide from the possible press pack that might want to interview us and take photographs."

"If any press people were here I would move away fast—I don't want to get interviewed," responded John.

"Mike and Paul are in cloud-cuckoo land—no one knows we are here," Ray declared.

I decided to make one last attempt to find a phone connector. I trudged back across the sand and into town and found electrical fittings in the basement of a supermarket. Low and behold there was what looked like the phone connector that I required. I was thrilled. After all the hard work involved with building the website I now believed that I would be able to upload my diary and photographs.

The non-bikers had disappeared by the time I arrived back on the beach. They had decided to explore further down the beach. Our team was alone again and it began to feel like we were bonding together.

We felt we should explore Biarritz ourselves, and strolled south along the seafront with wonderful white frothy waves crashing into the rocky coves. The temperature seemed about right except my sweat came out even when we had just walked a few hundred metres. "I can see why this town is known to be the crown jewel of beaches and has become the surfing capital of Europe," I remarked.

"It used to be a small whaling harbour until the fashion of sea bathing was introduced favoured by the visits of Eugenia of Montijo, Napoleon III's future wife," Paul responded.

"The building of Eugenia's villa, the summer residence of the emperor and his wife—now the Hôtel du Palais—definitely ensured the seaside resort's success during the Second Empire."

We wandered onto a promontory linked to the mainland by a bridge. We could look right along the beach, see the waves racing in and look back at the multi-storey buildings surrounding the main beach. Paul had intended to buy a digital camera but never got round to it, and used his camcorder to effectively take still pictures. He set his camcorder on a wall facing the waves and gently touched the start button then after a short time the stop button.

I remarked, "That's a bloody stupid idea. Were you too tight to buy a digital?"

"I never got round to it," Paul said, looking offended at being called stupid. "I never had the time to go down town due to work pressures." He often used his camcorder in this mode from this point.

Hunger hit us all at the same time, and we came upon a restaurant. "This looks like a nice sleepy romantic restaurant," remarked Paul.

"I will check the prices," said John, ever the accountant.

"It would be romantic if I was with a woman and not just you lot," stated Ray.

Paul laughed. "But you don't have a woman to be romantic with. About time you got one!"

We sat down and ordered food and beer but not wine.

"That attractive young waitress seems to have everything under control. Don't you fancy her, Paul?" I asked.

"Not today—I just want to get my stomach filled. You can have her," Paul replied.

"Thanks Paul for your cast-offs," I responded. "This seems to be like the lull before the storm to me. Tomorrow we start and there will be no turning back. The real sweating will begin," I declared.

"You're sweating enough now, and Paul as well. How you two will be tomorrow I just can't imagine," declared ice-cool John.

I walked back to the hotel to check out my phone connector. It didn't work! I assumed that there was just a possibility that the one that I had bought had a fault though it seemed unlikely. I jumped on my bike and cycled back to the shop and bought another one. Again it didn't work and I was getting frustrated to say the least.

Three days before I had downloaded the first diary entry with the information about the previous week and the present situation. I had then sent out an email to all my acquaintances that I rarely met but possibly might sponsor us (but they didn't—showing that the face-to-face approach is the only sure method of getting sponsorship),

"We hope you will sponsor our ride in aid of good causes. We have raised over £2,000 up to now. We expect to raise much more with our target being £10,000. Paul is expecting another £1,000 from his contacts, Ray is going round local shops and doing quite well, I hope to get more from Dupont-Teijin Films contacts (they have all been very generous), and John is expecting to raise well over £100. A prominent GAS-BAGS member, Zoe, has promised to double her sponsorship amount from £50 to £100 if we raise £10,000.

I am taking my laptop and am aiming to write reports and to transmit them back to the website, hopefully to add photographs as well. This idea depends on technology, as it may be easier to transmit from the moon!

The diary has started…see…**http://www.1bm.me.uk/diary_photos.htm**

Please can you help us raise more money by telling your friends about the website—whilst you are enjoying work, watching PC screens and having your daily drink of good

English beer, we will be soldiering on with sore bottoms, lots of sweat, and being forced to drink lots of water and a little French beer."

It was not that I really thought we would raise £10,000 but it was a remote possibility.

I also received an email from Bob Lappin, the Darlington & Stockton Times correspondent, who I now claimed to be our cycle ride correspondent:

"Good Luck.

I have sent the following for Friday August 20. They did put a piece in Town and Village on August 13th, but not 6th when I first sent it. I'll keep my eye on the web site and try to put some pieces in.

Once again Good Luck, I'm sure everyone admires you for your courage in undertaking this mammoth effort for good causes.

Bob Lappin"

I was getting worried—did this ride require courage? Not me! My sister and brother-in-law were celebrating their 35th wedding anniversary on Wakiki beach this same day in Hawaii, which sounded a much better idea than cycling across France.

Paul and I had brainstormed publicity at the start of the planning. The website was to be the centrepiece of the publicity and once that was built we could start to contact local newspapers and local radio stations. Paul took publicity under his wing whilst I was completing the website. He composed a publicity note and sent it to out to the Northern Echo, Teesside Gazette, Evening Gazette, the Darlington & Stockton Times, the Herald & Post (free newspaper), Radio Cleveland, and Tyne-Tees TV.

The Darlington & Stockton Times contacted us initially and arranged that Bob Lappin interview us. That week an article appeared with a photograph of Paul and myself with the heading 'Over-fifties plan a ride to remember' and Paul was claimed to have said, "We are all the wrong side of fifty and decided we needed a challenge that we can look back on when we are older." I must admit now that I never took on this challenge because I was the wrong side of fifty. I just had a dream of completing a long ride and never thought about being the wrong side of fifty. The article explained about the charities being sponsored but by an oversight forgot to include the website address.

Out of the blue we next appeared in the Herald and Post (again Bob Lappin wrote the article) under the title "Follow our charity trek", and this time the website link was given and the article also stated that a diary and photographs would be downloaded daily onto the website. I began to watch the sponsor list but no entries were appearing that weren't "owned" by Paul, Ray or myself!

I had now begun to believe that it would be easier to transmit back from the moon. I went down to reception and explained to the receptionist in my best slow English what I was trying to do and showed them my newly acquired phone connector. She said, in almost perfect English, that other people had been able to connect to the Internet with no problems and took a connector, which looked remarkably like mine, out of a box. She was confident that this one would work. It did and now I downloaded my first reports and photographs. We were live and our exploits could now be read across the World. Hurrah! I felt so pleased that I sent out an email to all the Great Ayton local newspapers and Stuart McFarlane and his right-hand man Tim Ellington at Radio Cleveland. I also sent a note to Paul's friends Nick and Linda in Australia, as Paul had asked me to ensure that they knew the website was up and running. This couple had promised to sponsor Medecins Sans Frontieres if we cycled the full distance.

Our expanded group agreed to meet at six o'clock to walk again to the Biarritz centre to eat dinner. We located an outdoor restaurant along the seafront, but then it began to look like it might rain. A waiter explained that we could move inside but the inside did not look very inviting so we gave our apologies, and decided to try Paul's favourite restaurant (with Muriel) in the main square. It was full so we went next door and moved indoors as the sky was turning black. Suddenly the clouds opened and rain came sheeting down. People began rushing around outdoors trying to find indoor seats. This was the third cloud burst in two days.

The wine and beer began to flow and we all became slightly inebriated.

"What about the waitress?" I said to Paul in a loud voice due to being intoxicated. "You must fancy her or is she too old for you?"

The waitress was very attractive, Spanish looking, black-haired, sunburnt, and brown-eyed but perhaps over thirty—not saying I studied her! We asked her to take a group photograph—little did she know that this meant taking photographs with Jeff's camera, Ray's camera and my camera.

Bridget, who perhaps was more inebriated than the rest of us, remembered the verse about 'When there were Two' and 'Twisted and torn testicles', remarked slightly slurring her words, "I would like to feel all your testicles to ensure they are strong enough to make the trip."

"You aren't feeling mine," responded John. "I'm not into these GASBAGS goings-on."

"You can feel mine," shouted Ray, "No woman has felt mine in a along time."

I smirked. "Does this mean a man has?"

Ray ignored this jest.

"I will have to feel them all again when you get home to check they are still there," laughed Bridget.

On arriving home (in Great Ayton) Bushy Ray, her husband, discovered an under-the-table photograph of my bare thighs and claimed Bridget had crawled under the table. I think it is much more likely that he was the guilty party.

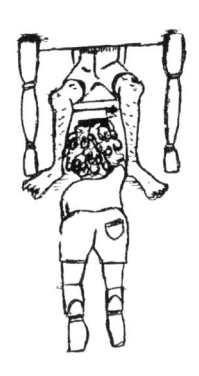

The rain had stopped by the time we had finished our meal, the streets were dry and again people were sitting outside. We walked back towards the hotel but when we saw a pub, the Mannequin Pis, advertising British beer we could not help but stop and have our last pint of good English beer and two bowls of chips (pomme frite).

# The Pyrenees

The French Pyrenees are dominated by mountains. Heading east from the Atlantic coast, the hills and valleys are wonderfully lush. The more the Pyrenees are penetrated the steeper are the valley sides (thankfully we would only be in the foothills) and the more gigantic the snow-clad peaks become.

The region is claimed to be more Spanish than French. The region's oldest inhabitants, the Basque people, have maintained their own culture, and their resorts of Bayonne, Biarritz, and St-Jean-de-Luz reflect this, looking to the sea and to summer visitors for their livelihood. Inland Pau, Tarbes and Foix rely on tourism and medium-scale industry while Lourdes receives four million pilgrims every year.

Historically, the Pyrenees are known as the birthplace of Henri IV, who put an end to the Wars of Religion in 1593 and united France.

The Pyrenees are subject to a Mediterranean climate of hot summers and mild winters. Summer is virtually without rain and except in the west, prevailing winds are light. In 2003 the temperatures reached over 40 DegC, which would involve tremendous sweating in my case if this temperature was reached again during our cycle trip.

### Friday August 20th

Biarritz to St Palais
40 miles Grand total 40 miles

I awoke early and began to think of the ride; 900 miles; how did I get myself into this challenge; would three weeks be exciting or boring? I had never cycled more than 150 miles on consecutive days before and that was over three days—would my legs give up? What if my bike failed? Should I buy a new bike or catch the train home? These defeatist thoughts spun through my mind. However the alarm sounded at ten to seven and we had to move fast. I changed into my GASBAGS short-sleeved shirt (I had brought two of these that were XXL size and fitted round me with room to spare)—I was determined to wear my GASBAGS shirts every cycling day. I packed my panniers and attached them to the bikes. I also filled my four water bottles, as I was keen to ensure I could replace my massive sweat loss.

I had been reading a book 'The Sun in my Eyes' by Josie Dew who travels all over the world on her bike. This book described one of her trips across Japan. She can be very descriptive and one passage was about her trip when the weather was very hot and humid, 'I'd forgotten just what fun it could be; constant rivulets cascading from temples; sticky tacky skin acting like a magnet for grime; sweat-soaked shirt stuck to back; tent like a sauna; sleep in a fever; a constant and unquenchable thirst'.

Help—this passage had made me decide to take more water as my sweating ability is in the top echelons. I decided to take four water bottles and not the two that I had originally planned. I informed the rest of the team but they decided to stick with two bottles each. Another good sentence from Josie, 'No matter that I drank more than a litre of water an hour, most of my weight was simply being sweated away along with my energy—a strange, blurry-headed sensation of evaporating completely away'. Yes! Yes! I had realised that I should come back much slimmer after all the hard work. I had bought two extra bottle cages from BikeTraks and attached them by Duck tape to the crossbars.

"What's that powder? Paul asked.

"It's GO Electrolyte. Roger at Biketraks recommended that I took it. I was going to take salt tablets but he advised against them. This is special mineral replacement powder. I bought two flavours, one blackcurrant and the other lime/lemon flavoured, at £6-50. Each jar makes up eight litres," I responded.

"That's very expensive,"

"It claims on the bottle that it's 'The Carbohydrate Energy Fuel with Electrolytes for dynamic sports performance in the heat'."

"That makes it sound wonderful. But what are electrolytes?"

"They are sodium, chloride, calcium, magnesium, and potassium. I did some more research after I bought it since I don't like being done though I do have a great trust in Roger's advice. It seems that it is best if you get sodium from both sports drinks and salty foods — as opposed to salt tablets — for two reasons. Salty foods stimulate thirst, and it is possible to ingest too much salt with tablets but very difficult with food. And then only if you don't think that your food and sports drink is providing enough sodium should you consider salt tablets."

"So how do you know how much sodium you have taken?"

I laughed. "A good question. I have no idea. Perhaps when you start to bonk."

"What's sex got to do with this? Does this GO improve your sex performance?"

"No! You're supposed to be a cyclist," I grinned. "It's a cycling term for when you run out of energy. Even Lance Armstrong has bonked—it almost cost him one of his Tour de France victories."

I went down to breakfast and thought this time I would have two boiled eggs, which you had to cook yourself in a special six-ladle egg cooker. I dropped one of the eggs in the water by mistake with no apparent way to fish it out until John came up with the simple solution of using a spoon—perhaps I was more nervous than I thought about setting out on a nine hundred mile ride with no backup!

Our fan club came down in their GASBAGS shirts hoping they could be included in the photo-shoot. I felt like a pop star as Pam and Bridget put their arms around and we all smiled into the camera—a definite photograph to appear on the website. The four of us wheeled our bikes to the front of the hotel with all the panniers attached. Pam then Jeff tried to lift my back wheel off the pavement but gave up under the tremendous weight.

Pam said, "Hope the bike doesn't break under the weight of the panniers and your tremendous weight."

"Would you like to leave your laptop here?" asked Jeff.

I grinned. "It will be fine. The weight will reduce as I leave a trail of sweat."

I tried to lift Paul's back wheel off the pavement and was astounded to discover that his bike weighed as much as mine.

"I think you forgot to take out the bricks you used for training Paul," I said.

"I have brought an enormous medical kit—it allows for almost any conceivable medical condition except childbirth," Paul retorted.

"You should have brought that as well with Mike's enormous stomach—he looks ready for twins," joked Jeff.

"I've only packed a few medical supplies including Ibuprofen, Canestan cream, Imodium and a knee support. I initially packed Contac 400 by mistake instead of the Imodium diarrhoea tablets, which may have stopped a runny nose but not a runny bottom." I laughed at my own joke.

"Why have you packed Canestan cream? That's for the women's disease thrush—and you look like a man to me," laughed Bridget.

"I have used it in France before twice when I got ringworm after staying in wet trunks too long," I replied.

"Sounds disgusting. Remind me not to go near you when you are sweaty," said Pam.

"You shouldn't be going that close to his thighs anyway," said Jeff, always very protective of his wife. "Leave that up to Bridget."

"What's the knee support for?—I hope you are going to make this ride," asked John suspiciously.

"Don't worry—it is just in case. I talked to someone at work. He recommended that I took one. He has recently ridden from Lands End to John O'Groats and needed one, but he did cycle up every hill including Hard Knot Pass and perhaps deserved a sore knee."

Jeff asked, "What is this?" as he pointed at tape holding a few spokes attached to my crossbar.

"I've brought a few spare spokes just in case," I explained. "I thought some spokes might have broken on the plane but fortunately not. Josie Dew wrote in one of her books that a bike gets treated with the respect that a bike deserves if it looks like a bike whilst a boxed bike gets treated with less respect."

"I can reduce your bike weight by taking them home," Bushy Ray came in.

"I'm also concerned that one or more might go on the ride. I know from experience that when one spoke breaks there is little impact and even with two broken spokes the wheel will only buckle slightly but once three spokes break the buckling becomes much worse and within a short time the bike is unrideable," I responded.

"It's very unlikely that spokes will break on a newish bike like yours," declared Jeff.

"I agree they shouldn't," I responded. "But when I first bought the bike several spokes broke within weeks, and unfortunately I was on the GASBAGS Men's ride around Beverley at the time. I had the offending spokes replaced in Beverley but once I returned home I took the bike back to BikeTraks who offered to fully check out the wheel and replace any more weak spokes. They claimed that it was a common occurrence for spokes to break on new bikes,"

"I think they were having you on," laughed Ray our biking expert. "I've never heard of spokes regularly breaking on new bikes."

"I found it incredible to believe but I didn't like to say anything to those biking 'gurus'," I replied.

Bushy Ray, was prompted to tell a story:

"My brother did a walk through a jungle in Tasmania, The walk was a one hundred mile walk and he had never done much walking before. The first day he walked fifteen miles with a massive pack on his back filled with tins of baked beans, tins of soup etc etc. When he arrived he wandered out in the forest and got lost for two hours, but eventually found his way back but had thought he was going to die. That night he unloaded all his tins and left himself with a tiny rucksack and finished the walk. That is how you will be".

At the end of Bushy Ray's long story he took a bow but we were all keen to get away in case he told any more stories! Both Paul and I had out our camcorders and we filmed each other filming the other. Bushy Ray asked the team to line up in front of the fountain in the centre of the square for a team photograph. Paul and Ray had also decided to wear their

GASBAGS shirt for the initial day whilst John wore a non-matching green shirt.

"Where are your helmets?" asked Bridget.

"We have to wear wide-brimmed hats to both stop the sun in our eyes and to protect our necks and we can't wear helmets as well or we would look ridiculous," Paul remarked.

"I wouldn't have worn one in any case—it is too hot and I told you I read an article saying they didn't make much difference," I said.

"Don't be so stupid. Crack a rock on your head with and without a helmet and see which is best," stated Bushy Ray vociferously. He had become a great advocate of helmets after falling off his bike on the GASBAGS's first 100-mile ride.

"It is more important to ride safely and not come off your bike—helmets make no difference if your head is travelling at more than 10 mph. I would certainly wear a helmet if I was riding off-road, and I am a strong advocate for children using helmets," I replied.

"An article I have just read by a neurologist and a concussion expert in the States says that even as helmets were currently designed, patients who were wearing them when they were injured were much better off than those who were not. The helmets serve the function of an air bag," declared Jeff.

"Well it is too late now as none of us have brought one and wearing a helmet does not prevent crashes," Paul replied.

"At any rate Lance Armstrong normally wears a helmet but ditches it in the last few kilometres of a steep climb," I said.

"Are you trying to equate yourself with a great rider like Lance Armstrong?" laughed Pam.

I ignored this question and remarked, "What do you make of my Tilley hat—bloody expensive—I bought it by mistake a few weeks ago."

"Why by mistake?" questioned Jeff. "I would never pay much for a hat."

I replied, "I went into the outdoor shop in town to buy special low bulk towels to take on the ride and spied a row of hats. One fitted my big head and so I put it in my basket. I was rather surprised at my large Visa slip that I had to sign and I looking down the list of items. I noticed £47 for the hat. I was astounded, gob-smacked, so much so that I paid the bill as I was thinking that there were only two days to go and it might be difficult to get a hat to fit my size head elsewhere."

"You do have a remarkably big head, no doubt there," retorted Bushy Ray.

Ray came in, "I bought a Tilley hat a few years ago and then lost it. I then went out and bought this much cheaper hat that looks almost the same."

"I read after I got home and took the hat out of the bag that it claimed these hats were the finest in all the world. I thought I should hope so at the price. I liked the guarantee as it said it is insured against loss, guaranteed for life and replaced free if it ever wears out. I will lose one every couple of years," I joked.

"I read the full loss statement which said that if your hat has been irretrievably lost, stolen or destroyed within two years of the purchase date, you may replace it with the exact same style for one-half the present catalogue price, plus taxes and shipping. So the replacement was still dam expensive so I took the attitude once bitten twice shy," Ray responded.

"Where's your black Stetson-type hat from Paul?" I asked.

"I bought it yesterday in Biarritz for just £10—much cheaper," Paul replied. "I looked at the Tilley hats in town and thought only a fool would pay that price. Oh! Sorry Mike."

Bushy Ray said, "Let's get on with the team photographs."

Jeff shouted, "Can you line up with your bikes on the roundabout. John can you put on this spare GASBAGS shirt."

John replied, "I'm not putting on a GASBAGS shirt—not after being called small."

"Ray and John—take your bikes—it will make a good photograph," Bushy Ray demanded.

Ray responded, "I'm not messing on with my bike—it weighs too much."

Pam joked, "Not as much as Mike's and Paul's."

Jeff said, "All look this way….that includes you John."

I said, "Pretend you are with us John."

Bushy Ray and Jeff flashed away and I passed them my camera so I could have a record to download to the website. However neither Ray nor John took any photographs, as they had not even brought a camera to record this life-changing event. When I later looked at these photographs John had either looked left or right but never at the camera!

Finally we were ready to go and we set off at half past eight through the streets of Biarritz. I had been expecting massive hills and being forced to push the bikes with all the baggage at two mph up the steepest hills. However the countryside was rolling and alike to Northumberland. The wind was behind us, and the temperature was not too hot. We were lucky. I wore a sweatband round my head and my hat tightly on. At one point I raised my tight-fitting hat to discover that a lake of sweat had built up inside.

I alternated between two sweatbands over the coming days, with the level of difficulty and temperature being the two factors in how many times I had to wring them out.

We passed a few sweetcorn fields and also a few sheep, which surprised me, as I couldn't remember seeing sheep in France before. I was also surprised at how lush and green all the trees and fields were as I had been expecting a more barren land—the rain we had experienced for the last three days must not be a rare phenomenon.

I raced along at one point so I could film the other three going past. John came first cycling with no hands on his handlebars.

I shouted, "Don't be so reckless! On second thoughts fall off—it will make a good film."

"I won't pick up the pieces," shouted Paul.

I shouldn't really have complained as later I cycled no handed. I had once cycled for a full mile with no hands and thought I was the GASBAGS champion until I competed against Zoe, who cycled three miles to my one and a half.

By twelve we had cycled 26 miles and had reached Saint Esteben. We stopped for a long lazy lunch at a restaurant surrounded by splendid views, lush green hills and white-painted houses with red roofs, a very clean outdoor pool, and perfect blue skies. The restaurant owner was keen for us to sit inside so she wouldn't have to traipse back and forth. We left it up to Paul to convince her that we preferred to sit outside. We drank up the ice-cold water that we were provided with in record time. No one ordered beer or wine.

I realised that I still did not know some of the background of my teammates, so to make conversation I said to Paul, "How did you get into cycling?"

This elicited a long reply from Paul, "I was born in Birmingham in 1952 and it seemed as if I cycled everywhere as a teenager. As I lived near the centre of the city it always required energy and planning to get clear of the concrete jungle of the West Midlands. I was always out with my mates of an evening or at weekends and also became a member of the CTC."

Ray asked, "What's the CTC?"

Paul came back with, "The Cyclists Touring Club."

I laughed. "I heard it stood for Café to Café."

Paul continued, "With my brother and friends, we used to plan long rides and also annual tours to Wales and Scotland as well as several English counties. I continued to travel by bike when I started work and rode a bike regularly up to getting my first car at the age of twenty-nine. While I continued to use my bike at weekends and for holidays, I began to rely more and more heavily upon my car during the 1980's. It was only when I got to know some of the members of GASBAGS in 1999 that I became keen again to cycle on a regular basis."

I shouted, "GASBAGS rules!"

Ray said, "What about you John?" to which John gave a much shorter reply—a cart and horses would be needed normally to drag much personal information out of him!

"When it comes to cycling I'm definitely the novice of the group. The longest trip I have ever ridden is from Whitby to my home in Middlesbrough, a mere 30 miles or so. I even caught the train to Whitby to ensure I could cycle the distance. Despite this, or perhaps because of it, I'm really looking forward to this challenge. You lot will no doubt have plenty of carrots and sticks to help me keep going when parts of my ageing body start to complain."

Paul smiled and remarked, "If you are lucky you old man."

Now I had known Ray for over nineteen years and knew that he had always been keen on exercise and used to fell run with his longest run being 29 miles. But I still did not know how he got into cycling, so prompted him, "Ray you old buggar, how did you start on cycling?"

He gave a concise reply, "I was a keen cyclist as a teenager, cycling to school, an evening paper round and many leisure activities which seemed to centre around our bikes. When I started work and bought my first car my bike was left behind at my parent's house and was eventually thrown in the bin wagon. I started cycling again in about 1985 when mountain biking started to become popular and I needed a new form of exercise that didn't hurt my back."

John interrupted, "What was wrong with your back?"

"I had back pain for years then had a disk removed a few years ago and could do everything after the operation. I was back to playing badminton and even took up tennis. Then the back pain came back and now my only exercise is cycling," Ray said. He continued proudly, "In 1990 I became one of the founder members of GASBAGS."

I was not noticing any difference from cycling on the right of the road but as we returned to our bikes Ray made a comment, "I will have to get used to getting my leg over on the right." He liked to make this sort of remark with sexual connotations!

By three we reached St Palais with bunting across the streets. I shouted, "Look they've put out bunting to greet us."

It's not for us," responded John, "no-one knew we were coming."

"Oh yes they did. I sent an email to Maite at the Tourist Office and told her all about our ride," I declared.

"You are deluded Mike. Look it says there is to be a festival that starts on August 22$^{nd}$," Ray laughed.

Paul said, "I'm not too disappointed, as this village is not twinned with any British town so I did not write to the mayor."

St Palais was a very picturesque little village with a claimed population of 2,200 but it seemed much bigger as it had an enormous number of shops, many more than Stokesley with its population going on for 5,000. Again the buildings were painted white and had red tiles and the same French music was drifting around all the streets as piped music came out of loudspeakers attached to buildings and lampposts.

The Hotel Midi, where we were staying, was located at the end of a square with a central island planted with trees and cars parked all around the island and the edge of the square. The hotel had excellent clean rooms with the Manager being very helpful, and at last in his wife I found someone in France who had read the website.

I had booked this hotel after initially finding that all hotels listed on the Internet were full. I had contacted the Tourist Office and within a short time I had a response from a person Maite, who had booked me into two twin rooms in the Hotel Midi for a cost of 44 Euros per room plus tax plus breakfast. This would be £15 each—very cheap. The email asked me to send an email to the hotel to confirm, which I duly did, and surprisingly no deposit was required.

My first job on arrival, after showering, was washing the biking clothes I had just worn and I stuck with this regime day-by-day afterwards.

Paul and I had brainstormed the list of clothes and other items we would take in our bike panniers as part of the planning. The number three appeared to be the prevalent number. We thought we would take three bike shorts, three bike shirts, three underpants, and three pairs of socks on the basis that one would be worn; one would be drying from being washed; and one just in case it rained.

Both Paul and I laid our clothes hanging out of the hotel windows facing onto the town square hoping they would dry. However on this day and most days afterwards the clothes weren't dry by the morning and our technique was to turn our bikes into moving washing lines by tying on the clothes as best we could.

I wrote up my daily report and plugged into the phone line with one of the connectors that I had bought in Biarritz. My PC dialled and I thought I had cracked it. However every time the connection failed. I took my PC downstairs and explained in broken English to the Hotel Manager what I was trying to do. I understood him to say that there was a block on Internet calls from hotel rooms, but said his reception phone connection would work. I tried it and I was through. I was joyous.

"I've cracked it," I announced to Paul, John and Ray who were sitting outside drinking beer.

"Cracked what," John asked with a distinct lack of interest.

"I've sent off the daily report with photographs again. I think I should be able to transmit most days," I exclaimed not put off by John's manner.

"You get your kicks from some strange things," remarked Ray. "I bet no-one ever looks at the website when we are away."

"You two are boring bastards," proclaimed Paul coming to my defence. "Mike's worked hard on this website."

We went for a stroll around the town and as we left we looked up at our rooms to see our shirts hanging out—the only clothes on public display. I called in at the Tourist Office to thank them for their help in booking the hotel. My Internet contact Maite turned out to be a very attractive young lady. She fortunately spoke very good English.

I said, "I didn't know if Maite would turn out to be a man's or a woman's name. Fortunately a very attractive lady."

Maite blushed. "My name means 'beloved' in Basque."

I asked her, "Why do all the towns have two names?"

Maite explained, "You are in the Basque country consisting of three French and four Spanish provinces. All the place names are given in French and Basque."

"So are you French or Basque?" I asked.

She replied, "I am French and Basque."

"Why are there so many shops in this little place St Palais?" I asked.

She replied, "St Palais is the central shopping place for all the local villages around here."

I asked her advice on where to eat and she recommended the Restaurant Trinquet just around the main square from our hotel. Paul booked us in then our Hotel Manager asked if we were eating in, Paul made the excuse that we were meeting a friend. I thought I must remember that excuse. The hotel manager would have been rather surprised if he had walked past our table, only about 100 yards away, to see only four seats.

That evening we walked discretely to the restaurant, ensuring the hotel manager didn't see us. Just after sitting down a faint drizzle of rain started but we decided to stay outside as our table was just under cover. A very attractive waitress served us but Paul was in stomach mode so did not ask her name or want to fantasize about her. She had alabaster legs, perhaps showing that like the Japanese, women who have the easy opportunity to go brown prefer to stay white. Our meals appeared and we got stuck in since we were ravenous.

Paul remarked after a time, "This is the best lamb I have tasted in years," and patted his distended stomach.

Ray followed with, "This is the best beef I have ever had," and burped which is his normal way of showing satisfaction (though sometimes he farts as well).

I remarked, "You sound like Jim. He always says this is the most marvellous meal he has ever had or view he has ever seen but then the same re-occurs the next time we are out." Jim is one of the ancient GASBAGS.

"The rain is getting worse. Let's pay up and dash back. Hope it stops by tomorrow," announced John.

## Saturday August 21st

St Palais to Pau
53 miles Grand total 93 miles

Again I woke early, half past three, to the sound of heavy rain and I found difficulty sleeping again. The rain went on and on and finally began to subside just when we were ready to set off, though there were large puddles on the road. The breakfast had been rather disappointing just being French bread with jam and coffee. I felt like Oliver Twist when I asked the hotel manager for more bread—he was sitting close by reading his newspaper, being uncommunicative as if he had noticed us eating in the nearby restaurant last night.

We had each bought the same make and size of rear panniers and now they came into their own. The panniers were made by Altura, and we bought the fifty litre (per pair) Orkney type, which are made of Dura-tec material, which was claimed to be highly resistant to abrasion and wear. We would find out on this trip. The bags were very easy to remove and mount. Inside the tops of the bags were bright yellow waterproof rain covers, which fully covered the bags. I had also bought the Orkney front bar bag, which was rather expensive for its capacity but very easy to lift off. Again it came with a bright yellow waterproof rain cover.

I had been keen to take the bar bag, as the advice from a friend, who had toured through France to Spain, was that it could be used to store all your valuables and be easily removed at any stop. Paul was adamant that he would not take a front pannier as he blamed having one on his fall when he broke his pelvis.

We fitted on the rain covers for the first time and then set off just after nine towards Mauleon-Licharre on Paul's scenic routes with good views but lots of hill climbs.

One of the early decisions that we had made was the route and we learnt that the direction of the prevailing winds was south to north so we decided to go in that direction. Our first thoughts were to get the boat from Plymouth to Santander in northern Spain and to head back from there. However Paul checked out the cost of the boat and we were surprised at the high cost (£88 each) and also were concerned at the extra time (18 hours) associated with being on the boat. Paul proposed that we check out cheap flights and found that we could fly to several places in the south of France by RyanAir, including Biarritz, and that there was only a minimal extra charge to take a bike. Overall it was cheaper (£52 each) and faster (3 hours) to go by plane. We thus chose Biarritz as our starting point.

When I first dreamt about going across France I had guessed that the distance would be about 450 miles which was only three times the distance I had ever cycled before on one ride and the ride was over three days. (I had also twice cycled just over 100 miles in a day but on fairly flat routes). I imagined coming up the French west coast on almost flat routes and staying more than one night at some of the resorts so I could peruse the talent on the beach (even at my age of fifty-four I still enjoy such sport). I had previously camped in many parts of the French west coast and knew that it was fairly flat though I was concerned about finding routes slightly away from the congested coast roads. However I have never been the one to volunteer to work out in detail a route from A to B, so when Paul said he would love to have a go, I thought wonderful. When I looked at a map of France it looked almost flat so I felt confident that the route chosen would not be too difficult.

Paul quickly came back with the idea to go east through the foothills of the Pyrenees and then to head through central France, to go through Ouzouer-sur-Loire as it was twinned with Great Ayton, with the final destination being Caen.

His estimate of the mileage was between 800 and 1000. He re-assured me that the foothills were only minor little bumps and I began to like the idea of seeing parts of France I had never seen. At this point I did not know that Paul had ridden numerous 100 mile rides in his youth so had no inkling that if

Paul had a choice between a flat or hilly route he would always chose the hilly route in order to make the ride more of a challenge and get 'scenic views'.

Within a short time Paul had the route detailed. The cycle ride would start in Biarritz and was to go almost due east over to Pau. From Pau the ride would head slightly east of due north in the direction of Paris before turning north-west at Ouzouer-sur-Loire (about 100 miles south of Paris) to finish at Caen. I checked the mileage on the RAC web site and asked for the route with the shortest mileage avoiding motorways which gave:

| Biarritz to Pau | 70 |
| Pau to Ouzouer | 409 |
| Ouzouer to Caen | 183 |
| Total | 662 |

However Paul was keen to not go along fast roads with thunderous trucks zooming past, and spent considerable time choosing a more scenic route that he believed would result in a route just over 900 miles, and had to further adjust the route to take it through the sixteen twinned towns close to the chosen route. I later looked at the maps and saw that they had scenic routes specially marked on. What I didn't realise at this time was the scenic normally meant climbing up hills.

The final destination was Pau and we arrived at quarter to six after 53 miles. I counted at least five very long uphills and an equal number of downhills on the way. The downhills were wonderful but I always knew this would lead to another long uphill, not that I am complaining! Along the route we had several showers so I either felt wet from rain or wet from sweat, but it is a feeling you get used to. I also became used to being at the back of the group when going up hills as my weight of 105 kg had a significant effect on my speed (or that is my excuse). Ray, around 75 kg, was normally leading with

John, less than 60 kg, not far behind, with any doubts about John's fitness having been dispelled. Paul at 83 kg looked certainly portly but could climb hills well due to his training programme.

I had known John for a few years and knew he played tennis but had been surprised at his fitness. As we cycled along I drew along side and asked him, "What sports do you do John to get you this fit?"

John said, "I love climbing and have climbed all 284 Munro's."

To me this seemed a remarkable achievement by the age of fifty but perhaps possible, as John has never married and did not have to bring up children. I knew that the Munro's were in Scotland but not much more. I asked, "What exactly are the Munro's?"

John must have known the background to the Munro's after climbing them all and came back with the full history.

"It goes back to 1891 when Sir Hugh T. Munro surveyed Scotland's mountains above 3000 feet and produced his 'Tables' cataloguing 236 peaks, which he considered to be separate mountains. That's why Scottish peaks above 3000 feet are called Munro's. He began a first revision of his tables, which was completed in 1921 after his death, and there have been several subsequent revisions. At each revision peaks have been demoted from or elevated to the status of Munro. Now there are 284 peaks but this number may change as clear criteria are still not agreed."

The views of the major Pyrenean peaks were spectacular with the tops of the distant ones covered in cloud, and on one of the hills that we climbed we seemed to be in amongst them. The first hill was very steep and at the top of it I was breathing deeply with the sweat pouring off, whilst Ray was still cool and said, "It was nothing but a molehill."

I remarked, "It may have been a molehill to you but it was a bloody mountain to me."

Paul arrived last, bare-topped and his hairy body on show, shouting out, "Did you have any trouble with the rabid dogs? I had to use my assertiveness training. They were showing their teeth and everything."

"Perhaps the dogs were frightened of you as you look like a hairy monster. Us three kept our shirts on and we weren't attacked," I laughed.

Paul had been planning to phone Stuart McFarlane on his Radio Cleveland show between eleven and twelve, as Stuart had agreed that we could give weekly reports.

When we had planned the publicity for the ride, Paul had been confident that he could get us on the Stuart McFarlane Saturday show as his son had appeared on the show several times because of his acting talent. A few weeks before we set off Paul had phoned Radio Cleveland and left a message for Stuart. A few days later Stuart contacted Paul about appearing on his show, and Paul was so thrilled he rang me immediately. The show was being held in the Redcar shopping centre as that weekend included Yorkshire Day, and the Radio Cleveland bus was to be based there for the day. Redcar had been part of Cleveland for many years but had now rejoined Yorkshire and had decided to take part in the Yorkshire Day celebrations, held each year on August 1st, with many other towns in Yorkshire.

As we drove to Redcar I said, "We should discuss what key messages we want to get across. I expect the main purpose is to prompt people to sponsor our chosen charities."

"I guess we also like the self publicity," Paul grinned. "I guess the key messages are that we are four over-fifties who deserve sponsorship as we are cycling over 900 miles. And we need to say about the five charities and our own reasons to support the charities."

"We must also give the website address very clearly."

"I know Stuart—he will repeat it again and again."

"What's Stuart's background?"

"He used to work for British Steel and started to work part-time for Radio Cleveland when he retired. His main job now is as a Radio Cleveland presenter. He also sings in a local Folk band, the Teesside Fettlers."

"I had assumed that we were going to be interviewed by a young presenter not an old geezer even older than us."

We arrived at the bus to find Stuart interviewing people in between playing music. He looked remarkably alike some of the GASBAGS members with a big shaggy beard, going thin on top and a slightly protruding paunch. He displayed rampant enthusiasm even though he must have been over sixty.

Just as we arrived I bumped into a acquaintance who I had often played badminton with. He turned out to be the one of the organisers of the Yorkshire day. "What's Yorkshire day all about?" I asked.

"As part of its efforts to preserve the region's Yorkshire heritage, the Yorkshire Ridings Society established 'Yorkshire Day' on August 1st 1975. In case you didn't now Yorkshire has over five million people—more than many European countries including Scotland, Denmark, and twice as many people as in Wales. The idea of a special day called 'Yorkshire Day' was to provide a focus for highlighting Yorkshire pride in the County. August 1st was chosen as it has special significance in the county's history. On August 1st 1759 soldiers, including some from Yorkshire regiments, who had fought in the battle of Minden, in Germany, picked white roses from nearby fields as a tribute to their fallen comrades."

I responded, "My own father used to believe that Yorkshire should have self-rule. He was born in Sheffield, and for all of the sixteen years he spent in Manchester he was a continual advocate of Yorkshire. Later he ranted about home rule for Hallamshire when Leeds was given a higher priority than his beloved Sheffield."

Stuart came across and we all shook hands. The live interview started and Paul started explaining about our 'challenge' and raising money for good causes. I tried to ensure that I got my fair say, giving my family background about my mother having Alzheimer's and stressing that people could sponsor us by logging on the website. We performed a good double act. After the live interview Paul pushed the possibility of us phoning the show each Saturday as we went across France. Stuart was enthusiastic so it was agreed.

I began to check the website to see if our interview had prompted a surge in sponsorship but not one unexpected entry appeared! I began to wonder how many people actually listened to Radio Cleveland on a Saturday at 11:00am—perhaps not a lot, with all the activities like shopping, getting prepared for football matches, and the other radio and TV programmes that were available. So to get no sponsorship out of a possible audience of fifty (perhaps I am being unfair to Stuart) did not seem so bad. However both Paul and I liked the idea of phoning up from France even if the audience was low.

To return to France! Now the time had arrived—we were going up one of the hills—Paul phoned Radio Cleveland and asked to speak to Tim Ellington, Stuart's right-hand man, but he was off ill so Paul began to go through a long explanation of who we were and that we phoning from the south of France and were on a 900 mile bike ride. I began to wonder how much this call was costing. Our contact said he would talk to Stuart and phone back shortly. We carried on and no call came through then Paul noticed that we had no signal—a possible explanation. We climbed up to the top of the hill and Paul phoned again to be told that we would be interviewed in five minutes. Paul kept his phone live as we listened to Stuart interview one person about his local football match then music played. The costs mounted but Paul waved away any thoughts of giving up now.

Finally Stuart came on air asking his audience (all fifty of them but probably a different fifty from the week before), "Do you remember the four fifty-year old men cycling across

France from Biarritz raising money for charity? Well they are on the phone now."

I could imagine all his listeners shaking their heads.

Stuart asked, "Hi Paul, how far have you cycled?"

Paul was off jumping up and down, "Hi Stu, we have cycled 70 miles…we are in the Pyrenees…we are raising money for charity…. please sponsor us…I have big Mike here."

I certainly was and managed to get in a few words about the website address, "Hi, please sponsor us. You can enter your sponsorship on our website…."

I was not really expecting any response again as only a very few of the fifty would be computer literate and probably those ones might be computer freaks and not care much about sponsorship.

Both Ray and John were standing many yards away so there was no chance they could be asked to speak. Finally after many attempts our voices could be heard on the radio giving 'News from the Pyrenees'. We heard immediately after the interview from Paul's wife that the 'News from the Pyrenees' interview had been very clear.

We arrived in Pau, with a population 87,000, and I could tell it was much bigger than Biarritz or St Palais. I had booked the hotel but had forgotten to print out any map detailing it's location. Fortunately I spied a Tourist Information Agency and was provided with a map. We checked into Hotel du Commerce. It looked very grand on the outside and had a smartly dressed concierge.

On entering our room, Paul ran to the toilet.

"This room's small and dark, Paul", I remarked, "What's up with the French? I wonder if it is to hide the dirt!"

Paul shouted out of the toilet, "The toilet's has a good light so you can write your report here. You will have to wear a gas mask though after what I have just dumped."

So I sat on the toilet to write my daily report. The smell was still percolating around, filling my nostrils with an unpleasant noxious odour. My knees were pushed up hard against the sink, as the room was minute, and the fan was rattling—not a very conducive situation to write a report to inform the world of our progress! I was expecting that the PC would not start up on some occasions, as it would be bumped significantly in my panniers.

I shouted to Paul, "My dam PC won't work—I will have to give it heart massage."

Paul replied, "It is a PC for heaven sake—you can't give it heart massage."

I responded, "It is just a phrase to describe the operation. I saw a colleague of mine at work perform this operation on an ICI-owned DELL PC that I was loaned and stood back in amazement when he first did this—I thought how dare he assault my PC! I need to press with some force on the keyboard a few times as the microprocessor can become loose."

With my report written and the photographs transferred to the PC I needed to connect to the Internet. This time the phones in the room were dead so I took my open laptop downstairs and looked forlornly at the concierge, gesticulating wildly as he could not speak English and my French was not up to asking about linking to the Internet. He understood and pointed to a connection close to the floor—so I sat cross-legged and linked up—my report must get through!

We set out to explore Pau determined to find the 'Boulevard des Pyrenees', as I had read that 'it has lots of restaurants and when the weather is really nice you can sit outside to have a drink just in front of the mountains and enjoy yourself with a very beautiful view of the Pyrenees on which you can see the snow till May'. We went in the totally wrong direction even though we had obtained a map from the Tourist Office, though it helped when we turned the map the right way round.

We eventually found the 'Boulevard des Pyrenees' and walked along the restaurants with food that sounded exotic but we settled for one that served pizzas. Now seated in the restaurant we relaxed, consumed swiftly two pints of beer each and even ordered wine. Across the road there were palm trees (Pau is noted for mild weather in the autumn and winter—It is claimed that the sun shines every day—except when it rains!) and various national flags, and beyond we could now see the wonderful views across to the highest Pyrenean peaks though a mist hid the detail.

"Those peaks look very high," I remarked.

"I checked them out", responded Paul, "The highest is just over 3,400 metres."

I asked, "I wonder how that compares with the UK mountains?"

John replied, ever a person for statistics with his accountancy background, "I have climbed the highest peaks in Scotland, Wales and England and they are like molehills compared to these mountains. Ben Nevis is 1,334 metres, Snowdon is 1,085 metres and Scafell Pike is 978 metres."

I videoed the view then interviewed each of the team, with Paul and Ray providing comments but John stared into the distance, not moving a facial muscle.

Paul commented "We have done very well, haven't we lads."

I replied, "Ok granddad! Our first twinned town and no bloody mayor or reception—disappointing!"

Paul said, "After all my translation effort as well"

"But the translation was crap so they probably couldn't understand a word," remarked John.

Ray asked, "Which town is Pau twinned with?"

"Swansea on the south coast of Wales," Paul replied.

I remarked, "I have never been to Swansea but I can imagine that it is a bit run down since they have a football team that dwindles in the lower divisions. However I shouldn't judge a town these days by its football team as Hartlepool has been transformed over the last few years."

"What's Hartlepool got to do with this?" asked Ray. "I know it is a strange place as, during the Napoleonic Wars, a monkey was interrogated and then hung as a French spy."

"Hartlepool used to prop up the old fourth division year after year," I replied.

I walked back to the hotel whilst the rest walked on for further drinks, and I spied an Internet access terminal in the hotel entrance. I thought I would check my email and bought a four Euro access card from the concierge. Within a very short time the terminal froze even before I had accessed the Internet. I complained to the non-English speaking concierge. He pushed and pulled it (and perhaps would have kicked it) and finally gave up. I asked for my money back, but after some intense gesticulating and hand-wringing, I understood that the only way he could give me a refund was for him personally to give me the money out of his pay. I felt embarrassed and I gave the poor man half of the refund back. I imagined that this poor man's pay would be very low and his children could starve because of me.

# Perigord, Quercy and Gascony

I had been to this region twice in the past with my family to camp in the Dordogne in a Eurocamp tent. In August 1993, when my two sons were thirteen and eleven, we stopped for six nights. The temperature was very hot and we enjoyed meeting some Dutch campers (French Eurocamp sites seemed to be split between the English and Dutch). We hired two canoes and zoomed down the Dordogne almost falling out as we navigated a rocky formation. After enjoying this holiday immensely we booked again three years later for two weeks on two different campsites (one the same as before). I can remember it rained and rained the first week, though this region is supposedly renowned for its mild climate, and this time we were surrounded by all Dutch families who now did not mix much. However the following week we had a good look around the area, walking round Sarlat, Rocamadour, and Les Eyzies. I took my bike on the back of my car and had one very tough but enjoyable cycle up the steep hill that leads to Domme.

The overall region is renowned for its magnificent beaches, expanses of pine forest, and dense oak woods. Castles, bastides and churches grace the countryside from Perigueux to the Pyrenees, from the Bay of Biscay to Toulouse and beyond to the Mediterranean

The history is interesting. From the coming of Christianity until the late 18th century, this region was the battlefield for a string of conflicts.

## Sunday August 22nd

Pau to Auch
77 miles Grand total 170 miles

This day turned out to be much harder than we thought as we started out at a quarter to nine and arrived at the hotel at seven with a one and a half hour lunch, thus over nine hours to ride 77 miles. However these 77 miles make the Lands End to John O'Groats cycle ride seem easy. It was like going across a giant ridged crisp with up then down then up then down etc.

I lost count of how often this occurred (later informed by accountant John that it was nineteen) but in the end Paul and I reverted to walking up a few of the hills on the excuse that we could enjoy the scenery but rather because we were knackered. I found it easy going on the horizontal or downhill as my weight plus my baggage was immense and helped the downward considerably.

I had begun to understand about the importance of lactic acid. I had always wondered what the pain was in my thighs when going up hills and I now know it is lactic acid build up. I think I produce a lot of it when I start to work beyond my aerobic capacity whereas Lance Armstrong's musculature produces much less lactic acid. His low levels allow him to metabolize better. In short, he can keep on going while I peter out quite fast. His low body fat scale at 4-5 percent range probably also helps his cycling as compared with mine which is likely to be up at 15-17 percent.

The first hill out of Pau was very long and I settled into a speed of about four mph. As I cycled up the hill my mind drifted back to my concerns when Paul and I had agreed that

Ray and John could join us. One concern was about fitness and the other was about whether both of them would accept that they would have a responsibility to raise money for charity.

I had proposed to Paul that we should raise sponsorship for the ride as I had a belief that there was more chance of completing a ride if money was being raised for good causes. GASBAGS had three times cycled coast to coast and raised money to support Yatton House, a voluntary organisation affiliated to MENCAP based in Great Ayton, and each time had raised over £1,000. (The first two rides had finished at Saltburn and when we arrived there we could look down from above onto the driving sea and the Ship Inn where a small crowd had gathered to welcome us home after a three-day trip. The awaiting crowd cheered us as we cycled down the steep hill towards the Inn). Paul was very supportive, as he had raised sponsorship previously when running the Great North Run. We brainstormed all the activities involved in raising sponsorship and again came up with a plan and list of activities: charities to raise money for; possible sponsors; sponsorship forms; sponsor Business cards; publicity including local magazines, newspapers, and radio

Paul's idea of going through Ouzouer-sur-Loire had prompted an idea. I wondered if we could take the route through several French towns that were twinned with English towns. I found a website that listed all the twinned towns, and voila! There seemed to be numerous twinned towns close to the rough route sketched out by Paul. I told Paul and now we began to dream of how the ride could be shaped around going through twinned towns. Paul and I both love publicity and now the ideas flowed: name the ride 'The Tour through Twinned Towns'; build a website showing a map of France with hotspots for the twinned towns leading to descriptions of each town; produce the website in English and French; contact the mayors, biking clubs and twinning associations of all the French towns to inform them about the ride; contact the mayors, and twinning associations of all the English towns to inform them about the ride; provide a means to enter sponsorship on the website; send all the towns contacts sponsorship forms and links to the website; build posters into the website that could be run off for each town showing when we would arrive there.

We had visions of being feted as we arrived in each town, being met on route by the local biking clubs, shaking hands with the Mayors, being given free accommodation and a handsome cheque to give to a French charity.

Now that we had committed ourselves to this idea we were keen to start some initial publicity by getting an article published in the Stream, the local Great Ayton Magazine. Paul's wife knew the editor and contacted her about the possibility of a full-page article on GASBAGS. I sketched out an article and Paul polished it up. The article was included in the Spring Edition and included the words,

"This year, the two of us, Mike Newton and Paul Greenhalgh, are planning to cycle through France from Biarritz to Caen in a period of three weeks, and the 800 mile route will include part of the Pyrenees, the Dordogne, Loire Valley, and Normandy. We want to raise lots of money to assist several organisations, which will include MacMillan Cancer Care Nursing, as well as the National Asthma Campaign, which Paula Radcliffe runs for in the London Marathon. Our cycling challenge will take is through many towns and villages, including Great Ayton's twinned village of Ouzouer-sur-Loire"

Help! I had thought most people in Great Ayton would have read this article, and had felt there was no backing out now.

Paul and I had decided about the charities that we would raise money for. The first two charities that we picked were

MacMillan Cancer Care Nursing and the Alzheimer's Society due to personal reasons.

Paul's father died of cancer and he was keen to sponsor MacMillan Nurses as his father would have required their help if he had survived his operation in 1995. Paul later wrote, "I ran the 1997 London Marathon with him in mind—he was also a keen cyclist and would have loved to have done a tour like this one. This is for you dad."

I was keen to sponsor the Alzheimer's Society as my mother has had Alzheimer's for the last eight years, and my father looked like he was getting the same condition. My mother had transferred to a Psychiatric Nursing home three years ago in a small village called Woodhouse Eaves in Leicestershire. I had been astounded when I first visited the home as there were so many old people affected by such dreadful illnesses. I realised that there must be a hidden army of these afflicted people across all of the UK and of course the World. I began to visualise all my present friends finally ending up in one of these homes, though I have now read that fewer than ten percent of older adults need nursing home care, which I presume means that the rest of the population die at home. I searched the Internet to check how many people might be in this hidden army and my best guess is 450,000 as there almost 4.5 million people over the age of seventy-five. It made me wonder if the Conservative Party leader was a regular visitor to these homes as the Conservative Party Conferences are always packed with old age pensioners!

We then chose the National Asthma Campaign, due to Paula Radcliffe promoting this charity as surprisingly she has asthma herself, and finally Yatton House, as it is in Great Ayton.

Ray accepted that he had to raise sponsorship, and I felt assured that he would. He had cycled on one of the GAS-BAGS coast-to-coast rides where we raised money for Yatton

House. He had actually raised the most by having the bright idea of going round all the local shops.

When Ray had proposed that John could join us, I invited Ray and John round to my house the following Monday to explain about the ride. Unfortunately Paul was tied up and could only pop in for a short time later. I explained in detail about the ride and our aim to raise sponsorship for good causes. John seemed to be keen on the ride and to accept that he had to raise sponsorship in order to participate. John explained that his job as an accountant at Corus was about to finish. He had been asked if he would like to take voluntary redundancy and had gladly accepted. He still had a few months to work but was prepared to tell his boss that he would be on holiday for three weeks. Paul turned up, accepted that John would come along and then had to leave.

As John was about to depart I said to him, "John, GAS-BAGS goes out every Thursday and Sunday. I hope you can come along. It would be a way for us to build some team spirit"

John replied: "I am quite fit enough. I don't have the time to come out as I am tied up in the evenings and at the weekends."

I was flabbergasted at this statement, so much so that I didn't say any more. I had assumed that John would want to get to know the 'Team' and I felt that we should get to know him before spending three weeks together!

I mentioned John's response to Paul and he was taken aback as well. Paul had a word with Ray who we think had a word with John as the following week, when I was not available, John seemed almost contrite and had become willing to go on some rides as long as it was not with other GASBAGS members. Paul had learnt in the meantime that John was renowned as being very sarcastic, and had become worried. However John raised this issue without being prompted and Paul felt vastly reassured.

When I arrived at the top of the hill out of Pau quite some way behind the others, I had a wonderful view of the Pyrenees. Paul was talking to a French cyclist. I was informed later that the cyclist had asked, "You are three cyclists?"

Paul had replied: "No, there is a fourth."

The Frenchman replied "L'Escargot."

My comrades thought this remark was highly amusing as it means 'the snail'.

The ride seemed to go through either forests of trees or fields of sweetcorn. Initially the only crop that seemed to have been planted was sweetcorn, a bit like rice fields in Japan, but as we progressed further there were fields of dwarf sunflowers. As we left Pau it was quite cool but as the day progressed the sun became hotter and hotter. Paul and I each consumed over six litres of liquid almost all water and no beer.

We passed a signpost for Condom, which is the name of a town and not at all to do with copulation. We stopped for lunch at Marciac next to a lake, where I stretched out my damp clothes straight away all over the bike, but nobody seemed to mind.

The restaurant was under a large canvas sheet losing none of the view across the wide lake. We each bought an Orangina. Suddenly a few wasps began to swarm around.

I said, "I thought wasps had disappeared out of France. When I first came years ago there were plenty and we captured them by using an Orangina bottle. But on the last few visits they had all disappeared."

Ray responded, "I haven't seen many in France for years also."

"I must admit I hate them—last year I was talking away in Ray and Bridget's garden when I felt something in my mouth and then felt a sharp pain—I stopped talking immediately."

"That is a first for you", said John, "Then what did you do?

"I felt a sense of desperation. I had heard of people dying from mouth stings by the throat swelling and blocking the larynx. I begged Ray to rush me to hospital in his car, as I thought driving mine would be dangerous in case I passed out. We arrived at outpatients where people were screened into urgent, see soon, non-urgent etc. I assumed I would be classified as urgent and rushed through to see a doctor, but instead was classified as non-urgent and allowed to go home after an hour as I was still alive."

"It is best to ignore them," John said unconcerned.

Paul was having none of that. He used his hat as a weapon and killed two.

"That's just made them more angry", shouted Ray, as he watched one start to descend into his half full (he is an optimist) Orangina bottle. He swished his hand above the bottle and the wasp re-appeared looking very angry about being disturbed from its feast and stung Ray on the leg. His face grimaced and I could tell he was not happy!

I said, "You don't look happy, Ray," to state the obvious.

Ray jumped up and began to probe his leg, trying to get rid of the venom.

Paul said, "I can suck it out."

'Totally-male' Ray, by now getting a bit frantic, shouted, "I am not having any man's lips on my legs."

John, who was Ray's roommate, looked very concerned, said, "Just calm down Ray—the pain will go away. Let's have a look."

John peered at Ray's leg, then pressed hard where he found a hole and out came some venom. Their bonding was complete.

When we arrived at Auch we had passed the point of wanting to look round the town until at least we had found the hotel. We realised that our instructions to find the hotel were minimal. I had not printed out a map as I thought the hotel would be easy to find as Auch only has a population of 25,000. Paul disappeared into a garage forecourt shop to ask directions, and strolled out nonchalantly after ten minutes sucking an ice-lolly.

I said, "What took so long?"

Paul replied, "There was an enormous queue. Then the assistant could not understand my French that well."

I said, "She understood enough to let you buy an ice-lolly. Did she not understand the number four?"

I thought the bastard, I had just cycled almost 80 miles, I was sweaty, my throat was parched, my legs felt like jelly, and my biking pal had not bought us all an ice-lolly! But my team spirit prevailed and I said nothing—I thought, "I will remember this!"

Paul ignored my question and replied, "She said go up the road and it is just on the right."

We went about a mile up the road and we searched round but there was no sign of it. We were getting frustrated after a long day. We all cycled back down the road slowly in case we had missed it.

Finally I asked at a beefburger caravan for directions, "Ou est Hotel Campanile?"

I didn't want to appear good at French, as I would get rapid-fire directions in French. Again we were told to go back up the road but this time we cycled past two roundabouts and found the hotel one mile further on. The conclusion of this to-ing and fro-ing is that we should have checked out directions better than we had.

The hotel was similar to the hotels attached to Little Chefs. There was a restaurant attached alike to a Little Chef but better as breakfast, the starters and the sweet courses were served as buffets, and we could eat as much as we liked (if all Hotel Campaniles are as good then I would highly recommend them for overnight stays).

I checked my emails and I had one from Naoko

"Hi Mike,
I read about the hard part of your adventure and saw Paul's face. He looks tired but COOL! Good luck from me.
While reading, I feel as if only Paul & you are doing the adventure….where are the other TWO?
Then a wasp attacked Ray….he was there.
Where is the last one?"

I realised I should include John more! I also checked the website sponsorship. The donations were growing slowly with two entries of £20 from two Dupont Teijin Films colleagues, and Paul's friends Nick and Linda from Australia had now entered £50 against Medecins sans Frontieres, with a message left saying that they were checking our route daily. We could now claim that the website was being read worldwide.

I was just about to sleep when I was struck by cramp. I have had cramp before, of course, but now I had three different parts being attacked at once. I had hoped that the special hydration powder that I had been drinking dissolved in water would stop cramp but I can report it didn't. I jumped in and out of bed with the pain.

Paul lay there gently snoring away with a serene smile on his face as I was racked with pain, probably dreaming of Julia and Muriel but hopefully his wife. I felt like shouting at him, "This wouldn't have happened if you bought me an ice-lolly!"

I lay there for a time, once my legs calmed down, wondering what we had missed in Auch. It seemed a shame to pass through a town without being able to walk around it.

## Monday August 23rd

Auch to Agen
57 miles Grand total 227 miles

Paul was still shaving when I was ready to go to breakfast and as I was starving I walked across to the restaurant first. Ray and John were already there. I remarked, "I had bloody cramp last night in three places at the same time. I had to jump up and down."

"Is this why Paul is not here? I bet he couldn't sleep," Ray said.

"He slept like a baby," I remarked, "—though a rather loud one." I laughed. "I'm always concerned about my 'PC muscle' on a ride like yesterday's. It was quite tough."

"That sounds like something to do with your computer to me. I can't understand why you brought it. It's bound to fail with all the bumping on the roads," said John.

"No, it's nothing to do with my PC. It stands for 'pubococcygeal muscle'. You must have heard of it Ray—you're a keen biker."

"I've never heard of it," replied Ray. "What is it?"

"This muscle sustains the pelvic floor, and stretches from the pubic bone to the top of the coccyx so can get compressed on a bike. This is also the muscle that contracts in the moment of ejaculation in the case of men or orgasm with discharging of the sexual energy in the case of women. A powerful PC muscle contributes both to enhancing the erotic pleasure and to the control of the sexual energy. There's a good article on the Internet about it, which claims that any man who desires to master the art of sexual continence should pay close attention to the exercises aiming to strengthen the PC muscle."

"What are these exercises?" Ray asked. "Why have we never been told about them?"

John laughed. "Perhaps they should be part of the National Curriculum."

"The first step is to identify the muscle. And don't try it here," I said glancing round wondering if this conversation had been understood. "You can try it in the toilet. You need to place two fingers behind the testicles, without pressuring. Urinate and then by pressing stop the flow of urine. The muscle that will become tense at the point when you stop the urine is the PC muscle."

"Perhaps we should start regular joint PC Muscle training sessions," Ray guffawed.

"I'll start watching for any inappropriate rustling of your sheets from now on," remarked John.

Ray remarked, "Of course the extra baggage weight that you're taking Mike must make a significant difference to your speed—keeping you on the saddle longer."

Paul and I had heavy-laden bikes whilst Ray and John had kept their baggage to a minimum to keep down their laden weight. I came back with, "A few extra kilos makes little difference if you take into account your own weight and the bike weight. It is obvious."

"I am sure it makes a difference to me", remarked John.

"It will make more difference to you as you are midget man—you weigh less than 60 kg and I weigh almost twice that."

"Stop being bloody stupid—any extra kilogramme affects your performance," remarked Ray.

"It's not a race—we are on tour!" I said, my voice rising.

Paul came in and supported Ray and John, but realised that we should maintain our team spirit and calmed down the argument.

I knew I was right as far as my weight was concerned. I had being cycling on a round trip of 30 miles as my training run. There were very few hills on the run just a few gentle slopes. I was covering the distance in just less than two hours.

I now packed my bags with all the clothes and other equipment I intended to take including my laptop PC. I achieved the ride in only a fraction more time that on my unladen bike.

We expected an easier day today as we had passed beyond the Pyrenees's fingers. We cycled back into Auch, and when we stopped at traffic lights I could see a magnificent stone-built building up on the hill in front. "What's that place Paul?" I asked. I always assumed that Paul knew more about France than me.

"That's the late-Gothic Cathedrale Ste Marie, which was begun in the late fifteenth century. It is renowned for having 234 steps that lead up to it from the River Gers," replied Paul.

John said, "I hope you don't expect me to climb those."

"Well I'm not—we have a long day today," Ray came in.

We had cycled five miles before finally we left Auch, and then we were off on a five-mile flat meandering run and I thought 'wonderful' as I more enjoy flat scenic routes.

Paul stated, "Much too flat around here—no hills to view."

I replied, "This is wonderful—more like the countryside around Ayton." I raced ahead of the pack. But then back came the hills again with a vengeance and our speed really slowed down and mine especially—perhaps the baggage was making a difference but I was not going to admit it.

Ray shouted as he raced past me, "See your baggage does make a difference."

Paul and John shot past as well. Ray's backside began to disappear into the distance as I went slowly up the hills. I thought though how well we were working as a team as we ensured that there were frequent stops to let everyone catch up—normally me.

Now the fields of sweetcorn had almost disappeared to be replaced by endless fields of sunflowers. We stopped on the way to photograph Paul and Ray standing in amongst the sunflowers looking like flower-power people.

"This French countryside seems to be just sweetcorn and sunflowers," remarked John.

"You look like you are having a wee in there, Ray," I shouted.

Paul laughed. "He almost did have one but I told him it might re-appear in his next packet of sunflower margarine. The sunflowers are harvested for their seeds and oil."

I said, "Did you see the ones back there? Some had almost died off with all the heads brown and pointing to the ground. It reminded me of the book 'The day of the Triffids'."

Our stomachs began to feel empty so we stopped for lunch at just before one o'clock after 34 miles, and for the third day on the trot the lunch took one and a half hours at the leisurely French pace. After lunch the terrain became flatter and we made an early arrival at Agen.

Just before we arrived John mentioned that his bottom bracket seemed to have play in it. Our biking guru Ray checked John's bike and diagnosed that the bottom bracket would need to be replaced.

I said, "John, I thought you had had your bike checked out?"

John replied, "I did but they must have not checked the bottom bracket."

Ray came in, "They can go suddenly so they may have checked for any movement and found none."

"Next time, if there is a next time, it would be better to have them all replaced as part of the servicing", Paul responded.

In the planning stage of this ride we had all agreed that going on a 900 mile bike ride required us to ensure that our bikes were in tip-top condition. I felt that I could do the standard maintenance like replacing or repairing inner tubes, changing brake blocks, adjusting this and cleaning that. But I felt safer if I left some of the more onerous jobs to the biking professionals. Paul and John had the same attitude. However

Ray regularly stripped bikes down, and I thought just for this reason alone it was worth having Ray coming along. Paul, John and I decided that we would ask a local biking shop to check over our bikes. I chose Biketraks in Great Ayton where I had bought my bike. The owners, Roger and Paul, are themselves great cycling enthusiasts and regularly take on long distance cycle challenges. I believed they could be trusted to ensure my bike was ready for this trip.

My bike is a Giant Central Park with 27 gears, which I bought in May 2002 for about £450. The bike is classed as an 'All terrain' bike, which means it is strong enough to go off road but is set up more alike to a touring bike than a mountain bike.

The chain on my bike had broken a few weeks ago when I was about four miles from home. My GASBAGS friends pushed me back home in almost as fast a time as if I had cycled myself—surprisingly with my weight. I decided to replace my chain with the best one Biketraks had in store in anticipation of the bike trip across France. As I had found out when I had previously replaced a chain, it was necessary to change my rear block as well. Now the Biketraks maintenance checkout found just one major problem—the bottom bracket was rusty, which I assumed had been responsible for the clicking noise I had heard over the last few weeks. The bottom bracket was replaced and now I felt my bike was ready.

Paul had a similar style bike to mine, but made by Scott, and which he had bought at Biketraks. However he decided to have the checkout at the local competing bike shop, Westbrook Cycles in Stokesley. John had his bike, a mountain bike that he fitted with slick tyres, also checked out at Westbrook Cycles. However, Ray fully checked out his 'Arthur Caygill' racing bike with 24 gears.

To return to France—we agreed to look out for a biking shop as we cycled into Agen. We cycled in along the Garonne River. My keen eyesight (with glasses or I am almost blind) spotted one. The bike was booked in with a collection time of ten o'clock the following day.

As we walked through the town towards the hotel I said to Paul, "What's Agen renowned for? It's looks to be quite a big place."

Paul replied, "It is known as the prune production centre of France. It must be about twice the size of Guisborough—getting on for a population of 30,000."

John continued, "Agen's prosperity comes from the famous plum trees that dot the landscape; the fruit is said to have been brought back from the Middle East during the Crusades."

I asked, "How come you are such an expert on prunes, John?"

"I buy them in bulk from the Asda supermarket. They keep my bowel movements regular. There is nothing like a good clearout in the morning."

"I told you about John's bowels and that he had complained about any thoughts of leaving the hotels early. He always said he needed a major clear out every day before he would straddle his bike," Ray remarked.

I thought I was back in hospital with this kind of talk—I had spent several weeks there where the discussion over dinner was about the solidity of one's stools. "Well I don't like them. Prunes were regularly served at school going back forty years and I didn't like them then and don't intend to try them now," I declared.

"Where is this town twinned with?" asked Paul, changing the subject.

"Llanelli in South Wales. It is very close to Swansea," I replied.

"That must be getting on for almost one thousand miles apart—an awful long way," Paul stated.

"It perhaps explains why I was unable to find any twinning town activity," I responded.

"Even the mayor is not very active—that's two twinned towns where we haven't met the mayor," John said in a relieved manner.

The hotel manager was very helpful in ensuring our bikes were locked away in a safe place, his garage across the road. We had found that each hotel was very helpful with the security of our bikes.

Later that evening we found a restaurant in a side street. Over the meal I remarked to Ray, "I couldn't help but reflect upon what went on our estate when your backside disappeared into the distance. It's surprising what sweat and exertion can make you think about."

"I'm surprised you talk to Ray at all after he went out with your ex-wife for a year," Paul said.

"I was pleased she was happy—I left her don't forget," I replied.

"It was quite a turbulent time on our estate," Ray said. "I thought I was the instigator of the events as leaving my wife left a vacancy."

"It all started way before that," I responded. "I think I was the instigator. It goes back to when I moved to the Skottowe estate in 1984 with my wife and two children. We had no roots at all in the north-east and I wondered how to get a social life. At ICI I met a colleague who was in the Round Table in Guisborough, five miles away, and I went with him as his guest each week for up to six months, but I could see that there was little possibility that my wife could get involved as we would have needed to have lived in Guisborough and we only had one car. I decided that I would aim to meet people on the estate. One of the first men I met was you Ray."

"I remember that," Ray replied. "Your wife met my wife because of having children about the same age, which led to us inviting you round."

"Yes, your ex-wife was always sociable. The next person I met was Andrew, again through my wife meeting his wife, as they had a boy and a girl the same age as our two boys. As you know my ex-wife is a wonderfully social person with bags of confidence and always found it easy to start conversations. I began to attend the keep-fit class at the local school and Andrew came along. Contacts grew and by the following year I had six men off the estate going to the keep-fit class and two, including you Ray, meeting us afterwards for a drink in the pub."

"What's all this to do with Ray going out with your ex-wife?" Paul said impatiently.

"I'm just explaining the background to what happened," I responded. "My ex-wife and I had always enjoyed staging parties with loud music and lots of dancing. We decided to have a fancy-dress party and I asked people from work and our new-found friends on the estate."

"We also enjoyed staging parties," Ray said. "There must have been quite a lot over the two or three years with everyone becoming friendlier and more intimate."

"It would be best if I illustrate what happened next with a few condiments—it gets quite complex," I laughed.

"I know a bit about what happened," John said, "but I would like to hear the full story."

"Here are some bottles—surprising that they've got all these English type condiments in this French restaurant," Paul said.

"Me and my wife can be the mustard sauces. Our next door but two neighbours can be the HP sauce bottles. You can be the salt pots Ray," I said laying them out on the table to reflect the Skottowe estate.

"Make my neighbours either side the tomato sauces and the tarter sauces. My facing neighbours can be the pepper pots," Ray said.

"That just leaves the ones who used to live where I live now on Skottowe. They can be the mint sauces," I continued.

"Do you get the picture of where everyone lived you two," I said checking with Paul and John.

"Yes, go on," said John showing keen interest.

"Well the HP sauce husband ran off with the tomato sauce wife but returned to their spouses after three weeks; the tartar sauces moved to Stokesley, just three miles away, then separated after a few years even though the husband was a lay preacher; the mint sauces separated and both re-married after a few years; you left your wife Ray and moved to Stokesley," I explained.

"Just confirm—you were the salt pots Ray?" Paul asked.

"Yes," said Ray and carried on with the story. "The pepper pots husband moved in with my ex-wife then returned to his own wife after three months."

"We forgot the Stokesley pair—they weren't married but were a couple. They can be the vinegar jars. Stick them one foot away John," I said. "The vinegar male partner moved in with your ex-wife Ray and they ended up married; I left my wife and moved in with the vinegar female partner."

"A year after that I went out with your ex-wife for a year," Ray continued. "Then the pepper pots husband did another flit and left his wife to run off with a woman that worked for him and then left her and married someone else that worked for him."

"It's hard to follow all this movement. It's never happened where I live unfortunately," John laughed.

"Almost there," I said. "My new partner vinegar and I separated after four years; you Ray went out for a year with the pepper pots wife."

"You certainly get around Ray," Paul laughed.

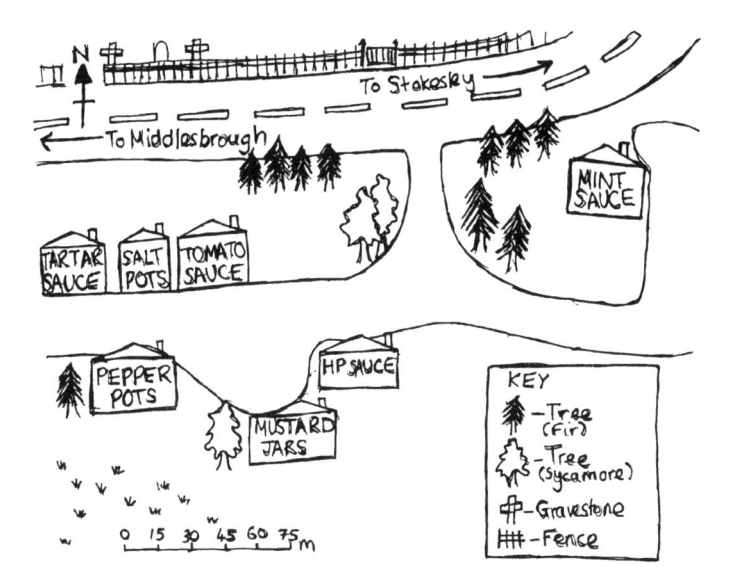

"What's strange," I said, "is that these sorts of goings-on don't seem to be unusual in Great Ayton as one day going back five years I mentioned to my physiotherapist that some affairs had taken place on my estate. She said I must live on the Roseberry estate as she had heard all sorts of rumours about the goings on there."

"I'm sure this is not just peculiar to Great Ayton. In my childcare role I come across lots of children from divorced families. Did you know that last year there were over 160,000 divorces out of 11 million married couples," Paul said.

"What I learnt from these goings-on is to never take sides, as it is not possible to understand other people's relationships," I said. "Fortunately that is the view of the courts in England and blame is removed when dealing with the division of assets. It is not like this though in Japan. There the husband either leaves and never sees his children again, or has to maintain his wife and children fully even when the wife is not prepared to work as any court judgement would leave him destitute. The

'Fathers 4 Justice' group should start a branch in Japan," I laughed.

I sent an email to Naoko in the evening, "We have cycled 225 miles which is a quarter of the ride and I am glad we have got this far. I have begun to feel that the ride is more of a challenge than enjoyment as each day has been hard. I will feel a real sense of achievement when it is completed but will I want to repeat such an event? I doubt it."

## Tuesday August 24th

Agen to Belves
59 miles Grand total 283 miles

Paul and I had decided to set out just after breakfast and then Ray and John could collect John's bike and meet us later as it was expected that John's bike would not be ready until eleven at the earliest. The first five miles were tough as the ride was uphill but then it became easier and at last the ride was as I had hoped. We were still biking between fields of sweetcorn or sunflowers and also a few grape vine fields.

As we cycled close to Villeneuve-sur-Lot, Paul remarked, "Villeneuve is twinned with Troon."

I said, "I know. I found a link to the Villeneuve-sur-Lot website on the Troon website. I was surprised as they are just over one thousand miles apart."

"It is an unusual place in that it stands on both banks of the River Lot. It was originally two settlements that merged into a single town."

We reached Monflanquin just before lunch. Paul remarked, "Did you know Monflanquin is classed as one of France's most beautiful villages?"

"It looks very picturesque," I replied.

Paul said in a plaintive voice, "It would be nice to stop here for lunch."

"We have not gone far enough yet. How about buying a Twix to share."

"They wouldn't have Twix's here!"

"Yes they do. I just saw one in that shop window. It was called 'La Twix' and looked the same."

"Why call a Twix feminine! Perhaps to appeal to a man's stomach."

"What do you know about Monflaquin? You seem to know quite a bit about French history."

"Monflaquin is a military bastide town that was built by the French in the thirteenth century on a strategic north-south route. It changed hands several times in the Hundred Years' War."

"What are Bastide towns?" I asked.

"I read up about these when I lived here for a time in my twenties. Both the English and the French, to encourage settlement of empty areas before the Hundred Years' War, hurriedly built Bastide towns in the 13th century. They are the medieval equivalent of 'new towns', with their planned grid of streets and fortified perimeters. Over 300 Bastide towns and villages still survive between Perigord and the Pyrenees."

"You keep mentioning the Hundred Years' War—when was that?"

"The Hundred Year's War started in the fourteenth century. It pitted England against France for control of French land, and had devastating effects. The damage of warfare was amplified by frequent famines and the ravages of bubonic plague in the wake of the Black Death in around the mid fourteenth century. France came close to being permanently partitioned by the king of England and the Duke of Burgundy. In the early fifteenth century the young Joan of Arc helped rally France's fortunes and within a generation the English were driven out of France."

"I always wondered what role Joan of Arc had played."

As we cycled along we passed another probable very picturesque Bastide town built on the top of a hill. We reached

Villereal. Paul said, "It must be lunchtime now. Let's stop here. This is another of France's beautiful villages."

We cycled into the village square, which was surrounded by turreted buildings, bunting was out across the street, there were flowers on all the window ledges, and the church bells were ringing. "This is very pleasant—it looks like they even knew we were coming. Perhaps we will have a welcoming committee and free lunch," I remarked, ever hopeful.

"You're too optimistic," Paul laughed. "That restaurant there looks inviting," pointing to one full of people sitting on outdoor tables with lots of wine on the tables.

We ordered delicious salads with lettuce, tomatoes and grilled goat's cheese on toast as we felt like a lighter meal and perhaps one good for our stomachs, but unfortunately we then consumed enormous ice creams, and for the first time we bought white wine with the meal, our first alcoholic lunchtime.

"There's quite a bit of wine left on the tables. It is like it is treated as water," I remarked.

"How about swapping our carafe for that half litre of rosy wine just over there—no-one is watching," Paul said.

"Why me? You've got legs—ok," as Paul frowned.

By the time we had swapped a few more carafes we almost didn't have legs. Just before we left the rain came again but just briefly, and now we were off racing drunkenly over the last twenty miles.

We reached Monpazier. "Is this another one of France's beautiful villages? How about stopping?" I asked.

"It is—there are lots of these beautiful villages," said Paul, "I think we should carry on as it is getting late and we will see another beautiful village when we reach Belves."

"Have you been here before then?"

"Yes. It is considered the most typical example of a bastide in the entire south-west of France and is very well preserved. It has remained remarkably unchanged during its seven hundred year existence. King Edward I of England founded Monpazier in the late thirteenth century, and it was only during the reign of King Charles V of France in the fourteenth century that the bastide became definitively French. It was one of the sites of the Peasant's Revolt In the late sixteenth century."

"You certainly know your French history—you sound like a talking encyclopaedia."

We hit a minor hill just before Belves and almost as if we could read each other's thoughts we jumped off our bikes and began to walk, not because we were tired but because we both had sore 'Biffons'.

"How's your biffon?" Paul asked.

"Rather sore. It was funny that year Doctor Paul came on our Beverley ride in 2002. I think some people believed his definition of the biffon because he is a doctor."

"I almost did as it seemed plausible. He seemed so believable when he said it was a well-known term for the part of the human anatomy that is biffed on as you bike along and enhanced his definition by saying it is just behind the bollocks and about the same place for a woman."

"Ray believed it so much that he searched on the Internet and got two hits. One was the GASBAGS website, the other was defined on 'A Dictionary of Slang' as 'the perineum—the place where the man's testicles would hit during vigorous sexual intercourse'."

We reached the medieval town Belves, with its seven belltowers, and located on a rocky outcrop. We headed to the hotel, unexpectedly to be met by Ray and John. "What are you two doing here?" I asked, "I thought you would be much later as you had to wait to get John's bike."

Ray replied, "The bike was not ready till twelve so we caught the train. You can't take account of mechanical breakdowns, can you."

"You mean that you have not cycled part of the route?" Paul asked.

"We've only missed a small part. I am gutted that we had to come by train," replied John.

"I will have to report this on the website for the world to read. Your fans won't believe it," I said.

"We don't care," Ray stated smiling.

After booking in, Paul ran off into Belves to film this beautiful village whilst I showered. I finally walked into the centre of Belves, through a narrow street lined with olde-worlde shops, to find Ray, John and Paul at an outside restaurant adjacent to the village square, halfway through pints of beer.

"Is that your first?" I asked.

"No, we're halfway through our second pints," replied Ray.

"You've got stuck into the beer fast then," I remarked. "What's going on here?" looking at the small crowd of people on the centre of the square.

Paul replied, "Shakespeare, a Midsummer Nights Dream, is to be performed this evening by an English troupe in English."

"Have you seen the notice over there in French? It says it will be understandable by the French," John came in.

"I find that hard to believe," I laughed, "I find them difficult enough to understand and I'm English. I went to one Shakespeare play and didn't know it had started until five minutes after the start. My last partner got annoyed at me when I rustled paper trying to relieve the boredom with a sweet."

"The covered market square is very interesting," said Paul. "It is 500 years old and there are twenty-three wooden pillars and on one there is a chain of the pillory where thieves and other bad citizens were attached. The roof is constructed from wood as well."

That evening we strolled back to the square to see how the play was progressing. It was being performed under bright lights since it was quite dark under the covered market. The audience looked to be rather sparse and perhaps not many more than the cast plus supporters. I couldn't see any French amongst the audience—well none wearing beret's with onions round their necks and quite a few were still white skinned and wearing white socks with their sandals—typical English! I wandered round the square, and stopped to watch next to one elderly man. He asked me, "Are you enjoying the play?"

No doubt English—I thought I had better be careful in choosing my words since there was a good chance he was connected to the play. "So, so," I said, "A bit different bringing Shakespeare to France. Are you involved?"

"I act as a chauffeur for the troupe. We all belong to a church and almost forty have come across to France to perform at a few venues. This is our third year."

"You must have great perseverance," I replied, rather nonplussed. Why make so much effort for such a small audience!

We all watched a bit more then returned to the hotel to get ready to eat. I checked my emails again and had an brief one from Naoko,

"Hi Mike,
Hope you sleep well without pain from cramps….maybe your fatigue beats your pain! Hopefully.
Keep going!
Hang in there!
Hope you don't want to do it again! (LOL)"

"The restaurant next to the hotel looked rather romantic in the moonlight. We can sit outside," John remarked as we came out of the hotel. "How about eating there?"

Ray chuckled. "Fine, but I am not sitting next to you. I don't want you to look into my eyes."

"It's odd isn't it," I replied. "Why does food always taste better at the place where you aren't staying? I normally don't eat in the hotel restaurant when I go away on business."

The meal dragged on with enormous intervals between courses. "About time we got served. This makes English restaurants look good," I stated. "What do you know about Belves Paul?" I said hoping a bit of history would pass the time faster.

"Its name comes from a celtic tribe, the Bellovaques, that settled in Belves around 250 B.C. In the 11th century it became a fortified city because of its strategic position. Under the market place, the Cave dwellings show how daily life was in the Middle Ages."

John came in, "Did you see the street names? Some have poetic names such as la Rue du Bout du Monde which means 'End Of The World Street' and la Rue de lâ Oiseau qui Chante which means 'The Bird That Sings Street'."

We finished our meal and we just couldn't attract the attention of a waiter to pay the bill. I finally got frustrated about the wait and marched into the restaurant to pay.

On reflection this day was one of the most enchanting and it would have been possible to spend much more time looking round the village. I would certainly like to come back again as Belves has olde-worlde charm.

# The Massif Central

The Massif Central is a region of strange, wild beauty and is claimed to be one of France's best-kept secrets. (This reminds me of the North Yorkshire Moors as we who live there like to think of this region as one of England's best-kept secrets). It is little known beyond its sprinkling of spas and the major cities of Clermont-Ferrand, Vichy and Limoges. The renowned Auverge, the lush volcanic core with crater lakes and hot springs, would be much to the east of our ride.

The Massif Central receives most of its rain in summer, usually as afternoon storms. During the storms, routes in the mountains can cloud over and cold rain buffet unfortunate cyclists (this did not sound very good). The mountains usually escape the heat extremes of lower places such as Clermont-Ferrand, where summer temperatures can reach the high thirties (I checked the map to ensure that Clermont-Ferrand is much further west than our route). Winds tend to be from the north from May to August and from the south for the rest of the year, though the mountain ranges create their own unpredictable currents.

## Wed August 25th

Belves to Collonges-la-Rouge
62 miles Grand total 345 miles

We were keen to get away from Belves early, as we were about to cycle through the Valley of the Dordogne, a very picturesque valley and expected plenty of stops for photographs.

As we set off Ray remarked, "You two must be cold," looking at Paul and myself.

I replied, "It is a bit cool, but our natural sweating ability under the least stress should make up for the extra layer. You two will get too warm soon with those jackets on."

It might have been thought that we were unfit and that we should not have attempted this ride with the amount of sweat that could ooze out of Paul and myself, but we had gone to the Well Man clinic just before the ride and been given a clean bill of health. Paul felt very fit and believed he was totally over the effects of his fall. I had had numerous injuries over the last ten years: bad back; Achilles tendonitis; knee pains. However my back felt fine, the Achilles tendonitis was reduced and my knees seemed almost ok. But just in case both of us had taken out insurance for going abroad.

The route was mainly flat as we travelled along the Dordogne River going past numerous fields of sweetcorn again, and through picturesque villages and past high cliffs. The first stop was Beynac in a car park. I remarked, "I remember stopping here about ten years ago. We went for a walk around and I bumped into someone from work. I had no idea he would be here."

"I've had that happen to me," replied Paul, "It always seems odd at the time."

We sat by the river for a time then cycled on. After a short time Paul shouted, "Let's stop—I want to photograph Beynac Chateau."

We all turned round and looked back at the crenellated Beynac Chateau high up on top of the cliffs. "You must know the history of that place Paul?" asked John.

"I don't know anything about it," replied Paul.

"That's a first," said Ray in astonishment, "You seemed to know everything about French history."

I said, proud of myself that I could still remember the history, "I went round it when we came here ten years ago. It's quite a long walk from the car park but worth it. The view of the river from the keep is stupendous. The oldest parts are built around the keep whose foundations go back to the twelfth century. The castle is protected on the landward side by double walls and ditches and elsewhere by the sheer drop of the cliffs of course. Nonetheless Richard the Lion heart took and held the Chateau for a decade at the end of the twelfth century."

We cycled past the bottom of the steep hill leading to Domme. I shouted, "I cycled all the way up that hill when I came here ten years ago. Quite a climb but worth it."

"Just tell us about it Mike. We haven't the time or inclination to go up today," responded Ray.

"The view from the walls is magnificent. It takes in the Dordogne valley from Beynac in the west to Montfort in the east."

"I've been there," said John, "I believe Henry Miller wrote 'Just to glimpse the black, mysterious river at Domme from one beautiful bluff…is something to be grateful for all one's life'."

"Who the hell is Henry Miller?" asked Ray.

"A great American author and painter who died in 1980," responded John.

Paul came in. "I know something about Domme. It is another bastide, built of golden stone and has medieval gateways that are still standing. There is also a large cavern under the seventeenth century covered market where the inhabitants hid during the Hundred Years's War."

"I remember that," I said, "We almost went round it but the entrance fees were too high for the four of us."

We cycled on and I powered away on the flat roads, but when I looked back no-one was following. I checked my map and realised I should have turned right at the last small village. When I arrived back at the village John was staring at his bike. "What's wrong?" I asked, "Another problem?"

"No—some bastard just reversed into my bike. I thought the French were supposed to be very considerate to cyclists."

"Any damage?"

"Only to his ears, though I doubt he understood my swear words. I think he just hit the bags."

The others appeared, surprisingly behind us. Paul remarked, "I stopped to take some photographs. It's almost twelve thirty. Let's stop for lunch soon."

"Souillac looks a good bet. By then we will have cycled 38 miles," I responded.

We settled down for lunch in an outside restaurant with the roof made up of branches full of leaves. "An interesting tree," I said, "Anyone any idea what sort it is?"

"No idea," responded Ray, "I've not seen one like this before. It's been great weather today after the cold start. I doubt it will rain."

"We've plenty of time," said John. "Is Souillac twinned with anywhere?" looking round suspiciously in case the mayor might have spotted us arriving.

"It's twinned with Denny in Scotland with 1000 miles between them. I couldn't find any mention of Souillac on the Denny website," I said.

"I wouldn't get involved in any twinning association with that gap apart," remarked Paul.

Just as we started off again the rain started and I thought I was back on Teesside where we had heard of reports of non-stop rain. "We won't rely on your predictions again Ray," John remarked.

We all changed into waterproof gear. I said, "At last I can try my new super-breathable waterproof coat costing £120 but reduced to £60."

"I'm also trying my new super-duper expensive rain coat as well for the first time," responded Paul.

Now the rain threw it down and everything was getting wet. "I may as well be going along topless as I am wet all over—on the inside from sweat," I despaired.

"I'm just the same," said Paul. "What a waste of money!"

"I thought I ought to enjoy the rain but I certainly don't. Just before I came away I read Josie Dew's book 'A Ride in the Neon Sun' where Josie cycles across Hokkaido. She claimed that she enjoyed the continual downpours," I said.

"Women are strange creatures," responded John.

"Have you got the hots for Josie? You keep mentioning her," Paul grinned.

"She is very attractive. And I'm very impressed with her life style. She's been cycling round the world for the last twenty years, since the age of sixteen," I responded.

The rain finally stopped as we neared Turenne. Paul exclaimed, "Let's go and get a hot chocolate and a Twix."

Ray looked at the clouds and declared, "It will start again soon."

"You were wrong last time Ray. I need food inside me," Paul responded forlornly.

"I'm with Ray," said John, ever supportive of his mountain bike partner.

"Me too," I said.

So we went on, and he was right as we again hit more rain.

John knew the Guesthouse 'La Vigne Grande' was two and a half kilometres from Collonges-la-Rouge but had no idea in which direction. Fortunately it was on our route and we arrived in this out-in-the-country guesthouse, with wonderful views, and an enormous dog that came yapping at Paul's heels. "He must have learnt about your hairy chest from those other dogs," I laughed.

A big wide man in shorts and sandals appeared at the doorway. Paul approached him speaking his best French. However the man responded in perfect English with a French accent, "You must be the four crazy cyclists. I am the owner.

Welcome! My name is Pierre. I see you have met my dog—he especially likes men with a strong masculine smell," and he laughed. We learnt later that he was married to a Geordie and often visited England.

The Guesthouse did not serve an evening meal so it was necessary to go into Collonges-la-Rouge, and the group decided to go by foot as everyone had had enough of biking! However I stopped on to update the website. I asked Pierre if I could plug into his downstairs phone line. I had a chat with Pierre. He knew a lot about IT systems and had built the website for his Guesthouse.

After uploading my story I checked for sponsorship on the French and Japanese legs, which had been added after the English leg was finalised. Paul and I had realised that there was little possibility that the French would sponsor English charities—would we sponsor French charities!—so we had found French charities for the French leg of the website: 'Medecins sans Frontieres' and 'France Alzheimer et Maladies Apparentées'. Naoko had come up with a list of Japanese charities: 'Japanese Asthma Society' and the 'Japanese National Cancer Centre'.

There was still only the one entry of Paul Le Velo on the French leg. I also checked to see if we had received any Japanese sponsorship though Naoko thought it would be very unlikely that there would be any as the Japanese do not raise sponsorship for charities this way. Charities normally receive money from the state. I was working for Dupont Teijin Films that had Manufacturing sites in Japan with over 300 people that I could access through the email address book. I had been thinking to send them all an email about our cycling challenge but I lost my nerve and finally sent a note to a key IT Manager in Japan to get his advice. I never received a reply.

Sending to the website took more time than I thought so I shot down the hill on bike forgetting my lights, missed a turn, came back, went through a wood, and after a few more turns finally arrived at houses which I hoped was Collonges-la-Rouge. The place was aptly named as the buildings were built of carmine sandstone and looked quite beautiful for an individual house, though the overall effect took some time getting used to, for it was both austere and fairytale like. As I biked through the village looking for the others, a beautiful young French woman ran out and gestured me to come down to her cellar.

I thought it's my turn for a woman—that's one in the eye for Paul—and was all ready for an interesting romantic evening. But then I found Paul, Ray and John downstairs. "Where have you been?" they all shouted.

"I was delayed updating the website," I responded, "So I came down on my bike."

"We've been waiting to place our order for the last half an hour," Paul said.

"You don't look like you've missed out on the beer. You seem well-oiled."

"Just our third pint," Ray laughed.

The night wore on and as I had my bike I set off first little realising how dark it could be without lights. I cycled back up to the main road then turned right to go down to the wood. It was pitch dark when I entered the wood since there was no moon, and I became very apprehensive about continuing, realising that one false turn could get me lost for the night. I thought about turning and going back to the restaurant to join up with the others but what if they had gone a different way. I thought back to the turns I had taken on the way down—could I repeat them in reverse? It was not safe to cycle so I dismounted from my bike and walked quickly looking at the faint skyline. I could see me going round and round in the dark all night. Beads of perspiration appeared on my brow though the evening was quite cool. I took a left turn, then a right turn, then another left turn then the path began to rise and at last I recognised the path and after ten more minutes arrived back at the Guesthouse. I put on a nonchalant air when the other three arrived back at the hotel after a half hour walk, also without lights. They were fortunate that the moon came out.

## Thurs August 26th

Collonges-la-Rouge to Treignac
49 miles Grand total 394 miles

The rain came again in the night but by the time we were due to set off it had stopped. I was hoping for a gentle flat ride as we had had along the Dordogne River, but soon we were cycling up a long slow road to a peak, then there was a wonderful four and a half mile drop into Brive. Paul remarked, "That was the best hill down into a town I have ever cycled."

"This sounds like one more of Jim's 'best' tales. Are you sure that that's the best one in your life?" I asked smiling.

"Ok—I do remember a better one going back a few years in Scotland," Paul laughed.

I said, "I really enjoy swooping fast down hills now but on my first cycle down a steep hill at the age of twelve I ended up full of cuts and grazes. I lived in Flixton, near Manchester, which is a very flat area."

"I didn't know you had lived near Manchester. I thought you were Yorkshire through and through. I lived near Manchester for a time," Paul responded

"Both of my parents were born in Sheffield but they moved to Manchester just after the war due to my dad's work. So I was born a Lancastrian meaning I couldn't play for the Yorkshire cricket team much to my dad's disappointment."

"I didn't know you were good at cricket?"

"I'm not but if I had been then I would have been snookered—playing cricket for Yorkshire would not have been on the agenda."

John laughed. "What's snooker got to do with cricket?"

I ignored this remark and continued, "To get back to what I was saying. One weekend we drove across to Sheffield to see my dad's brother's family. My cousin Peter, one year older than me, suggested that we should go on a bike ride. I borrowed his sister's bike and he led me down Twentywell Lane, which must be one of the steepest hills in England."

"Not as steep as Rosedale Chimney," Ray interrupted, "I've cycled up that one."

"He shouted go faster as he often cycled down this hill. I had no idea where I was so I tried to keep up with him. My bike started twitching and then I was thrown onto the road, receiving cuts and grazes to my knees, elbows and hips. I met my cousin again just a few weeks ago and he said he still feels guilty every time he goes down that hill now. However that incident gave me respect for biking at speed and made me more aware of the consequences of hitting the ground when going fast. So I think it was a lesson well learnt."

Our route took us just on the outskirts of Brive. I could see that the houses were similar to ones we had seen at Biarritz but now the roofs were brown rather than red. I shouted to Paul as we cycled along, "Quite funny. When I translated the full name of Brive to English with Google it translated 'Brive-la-Gaillarde' to 'Brive-the-Strapping woman'."

"Brive is classed as one of the five most beautiful villages of France. A shame we are bypassing it," remarked Paul. "It's twinned with Dunstable—I would enjoy exchanging with this place."

"I checked on the Internet to see if they exchange. Both towns have excellent websites but make no mention of twinning," I said.

John cycled up. "Did you mention twinning? We had better get going faster up this hill in case we are chased by the mayor," he laughed.

The exhilarating downhill was followed by a four-mile climb out of Brive, and again I saw three bottoms disappearing into the distance with Ray's in the lead. We were now cycling up and down hills again and again, which I guess was not too surprising as we were passing through the Massif Central.

We cycled through Tulle, which looked to be a strange, unattractive-looking place. It was strung out along the bottom of the narrow and deep valley of the Corrèze, and it looked grey, run-down and industrial. "Wasn't Tulle another of the twinned towns we aimed to pass through?" Paul asked.

"Yes it is twinned with Bury in Lancashire—a rather run-down town," I replied.

"That's the place that recently had race riots isn't it?" Ray asked.

Paul replied, "I didn't think you read newspapers or watched the news Ray. Yes you are right." Ray always boasted that he had never voted in his life so it was assumed that he probably didn't take much interest in the daily news.

"This place looks to be as rough and industrialised though so perhaps they are well matched," I said.

"This is not the best part of Tulle. I stayed here years ago. When you go down to the riverside and the area around the cathedral, it is full of fascinating winding lanes and stairways bordered by very handsome houses—many as old as the fourteenth century—with an imposing Hôtel de Ville at the end of the main commercial street," Paul stated. He continued, laughing, "We could call in and see the mayor—check if he received my letter."

"I'm not going anywhere near the town hall. We need to get on with the ride," remarked Ray, always keen to reach the destination.

"It's a shame that we can miss some of the main sights when the aim is to reach a destination. We should spend more time looking round," I responded.

"Well you two can go and look round and meet the mayor but we're cycling on," said John, speaking for Ray and himself.

So we cycled on. Ray remarked after a few miles, "That's odd—my speedometer is acting up. It keeps dropping down to zero then resuming again."

"Mine's doing the same," I said.

"Mine's fine," remarked Paul.

"Both Mike's and mine transmit a signal with a transmitter on the front forks to the speedometer on the handlebars but yours is linked via a wire," Ray advised.

"How odd," I exclaimed, "What could cause this interference? There are no electrical cables around and no houses in sight."

"It must be strong radiation! Could this phenomenon be affecting our brains as well? Or other parts? Perhaps we will go sterile," John looked perturbed.

"It too late for me—I was chopped off a few years ago," I laughed.

"And me," said Paul.

"I was chopped off straight after we had our two girls," Ray said. "I can't see why you care John—you don't want children."

"I just like to be whole," replied John.

After a few miles both speedometers resumed their normal operation. Strange!

We stopped for lunch at Seilhac in a small pavement restaurant. Each of us chose the fixed ten Euro menu of Pâté, followed by two rolled crepes with cheese and chips, followed by pear cake, followed by coffee, plus as much bread as we could eat and four carafes of cold water. We all left a tip, as the food was very good value, and the service by the French waitress excellent.

Paul had been studying the map. "I want to cycle via the marked scenic route. There should be some good photographic opportunities. There is a shorter route to the guesthouse if anyone wants to go straight there."

"I'm going straight there—I've seen enough scenic views today," responded Ray.

"I'm joining you Ray," said John, ever supportive of his room-sharing mate.

"I'll join you Paul," I said, without a great deal of enthusiasm as I felt I had seen enough scenic views. But I thought I should accompany Paul rather than him going off by himself.

We shot down a hill till we arrived at a bridge over a river. "This is the scenic bit," said Paul.

"Is it?" I asked, looking round. "It just looks like a bridge over a river to me."

We stopped for a short time to take some photographs with first Paul on the scenic bridge then me on the scenic bridge. We even stopped a cyclist so we could have a photograph of Paul and myself on the scenic bridge! However there was now a steep climb up to Treignac and I doubt the scenic view warranted the effort. For once I kept on my bike at a crawling speed with no view of bottoms in front as Paul had decided to walk. I arrived at the top of the hill and lay back for ten minutes waiting for Paul, the soporific heat consuming me.

We cycled down to the booked accommodation that was at Maury near Affieux, just outside Treignac. The accommodation was in a Gites de France country home, which was an enormous grey stone building with high peaked roofs and white shutters on all the windows.

John had booked this accommodation, and it looked more interesting than our previous hotel stays. Paul and I had decided that booking the accommodation booking could be left till late in our plan in part because we felt there would be sufficient accommodation on the chosen route but also we had a dream of being provided with free accommodation once the mayors of the twinned towns had read our letters and emails to them.

Paul had taken on the action of writing to the mayors and sent out a standard letter to each of them. The letter stated that we were four cyclists touring through French twinned towns and would they like to help raise money for good causes and provide advice on booking accommodation. We also asked if they could provide contact details for the Twinning association and the local biking group. We had waited expectantly for the replies to come back. A week went by, then two, then three and we realised that we unlikely to get much of a response.

Paul and I had both bought the Lonely Planets book 'Cycling through France' which had a section on 'Accommodation'. The first 100 or so pages detailed 'Facts for the Cyclist' and 'Health and Safety' of which some sections were very useful but I was less interested in other sections like 'Gay & Lesbian Cyclists' and 'Women's Health'. Unfortunately the other 400 pages proposed cycling routes in all the regions of France but had little relevance to the route that we aimed to travel.

Fortunately it worked out that Ray and John had signed up by the time the accommodation had to be booked but then Ray had to go away with work for a few weeks so the hotel booking was split three ways. Paul and I both had home PC's but John needed to book on his PC at work. John set to straight away and raised our confidence in his involvement. He sent us a list of possible sites to use. Paul and I took the easy path and used hotel chain websites, Logis Europe and Hotel Campanile. John took a different route to booking accommodation. He used the Chambres D'Hote and Gites de France websites that provided for booking guesthouse and B&B type accommodation. I would like to believe that he took this path because he wanted to be more adventurous and to move away from the standard hotel scene where there would be little chance of meeting new people. However I think it is more likely his concern was to do with the price. The accommodation, he chose however, did turn out to be the most interesting, though located away from the town centres.

Whilst John was pulling his weight as regards booking accommodation, Paul and I were concerned about his pledge to raise sponsorship. Ray, though he had openly accepted that he had to raise sponsorship, questioned Paul to see if this was just my idea but Paul re-assured him that he was equally committed to raise as much as possible. Ray had been sure that none of his friends would enter sponsorship directly on the website, and suddenly added a flurry of entries himself with names like "Pat & Nickie, "Dav & Fi". None of these people were known to the rest of us. Would we ever be able to collect this money if Ray was knocked down and killed on the ride? Had he thought of this possibility? Ray had tried to get sponsorship from the local shops with less success this time than his previous effort some years ago.

Paul and I began to get very frustrated with John, though we tried not to show it to keep up a good team spirit. John had not entered sponsorship on the website with only three weeks before the start date. He had not even sponsored any of the charities himself. Paul and I felt aggrieved, as we had agreed that John could come along only if he raised sponsorship. At the weekly meeting with three weeks to go, I tried the embarrassment technique. "How much have you raised Paul," I asked.

Paul knew what was going on so enthusiastically said, "I've now raised over £1,000 and entered it all on the website. I'm hoping to raise much more from my solicitor friends. I have sent each practice a sponsorship form and hope to get them back soon."

"What about you Ray?" I asked.

"I've almost raised £250 and entered it all on the website. I am hoping to get a bit more," he replied.

"I've raised about £700. I'm still going round people at work. It takes time," I stated, then added, "What about you John? There's only three weeks to go."

All eyes stared at John. He frowned then stated, "I am hoping to get some sponsorship. I have been pledged some."

"Can you enter it on the website then so we can assess the total?" I asked.

John muttered something, which I understood to mean he would try. I watched the website day by day but John did not enter anything. With a week to go Paul and I agreed that he would try this time at our weekly meeting. Paul was very positive about how much we had raised to this point, over £2,000, and prompted John to add his sponsorship so we could get over £2,500 before the ride. John nodded, said he hoped to. Ray remarked, "Even your sister has added some sponsorship."

However by the time the ride started John had entered no sponsorship. Paul and I felt even more aggrieved but decided that we must not let John's lack of commitment to sponsorship affect our enjoyment of the ride.

Odile, the owner of the house and an attractive dark-haired woman in her early forties, came out and gave us a can of lager each and we sat back admiring the view across the immense lawns. I said, "An excellent view, Paul."

"She's not my type," Paul stated, "A bit frumpish for me!"

"You have a one-track mind, Paul. I meant the view of the hills not Odile's disappearing backside. I think she looks very pleasant."

Odile re-appeared after a short time and led us round the side and up some outdoor stairs to a large bedroom. There were some training shoes on the floor, which turned out to be Ray's. Odile explained in French that we would share a common bathroom with Ray and John, which was the link room between the two bedrooms. Ray and John had arrived quite some time before and had had a bath (there was no shower). I went to get one and John remarked, "You will have to be a contortionist to fit in it!" as I looked down at the bath that was about three foot long.

"It looks like it's been sized for the smaller-sized people when the house was built several centuries ago. I guess you fitted John," I laughed.

John replied, "We aren't all as tall as you—you long piece of string! The bath is actually relatively new—you can tell from the material."

I washed my clothes and hung them on the outside balcony leading to the rooms. We had so much space that it was wonderful—the odd thing was that the clothes did not dry at all. In the hotel rooms there had been the same problem but even here the late afternoon sun had no drying ability.

I wrote up my report and transferred photographs from my camera to the PC. There was no phone in the rooms so I knocked on the back door, and Odile led me into a massive kitchen, where she was preparing dinner. I plugged in and our latest exploits hit the world at large. Whenever I had asked to access the Internet this way, nobody had asked me whether I was phoning a local or an international line, and I had also not been charged for making the Internet calls as of yet. I was actually phoning a local phone number because of the use of the Net2Roam service.

I went outside to admire the view from the massive lawned garden surrounded by pine trees with a gap through to provide a view that looked across distant hills. There was a large red children's paddling pool in the garden. We had all assumed that pool was not for us but we had seen no children around. The other three were lying on the lawn trying to get the last rays of sunshine.

That evening we were served a superb meal by Odile, which included two carafes of wine all for the price of eleven euros each. The meal consisted of pate (many French meals seem to start with pate), noodles plus sauce, followed by cheese, followed by a fruit pie.

Paul and I had been speculating that the house could be three or four hundred years old and Paul thought perhaps a retreat of Louis V's. We checked with Odile and it turned out to have been built around 1805. Odile did not speak English but I understood enough of her explanation of the house ownership. Her husband and herself had bought the house a few years ago. He worked part time as a doctor and spent the rest of his time improving the house. The guesthouse business was Odile's responsibility.

By the time we finished dinner it was past nine o'clock. Ray remarked, "It's too late to go and investigate Treignac now."

"It's only a few kilometres down the road. It would be good to look round. It is a medieval village that again belongs to 'the most beautiful villages of France' club. The parish church goes back to the eleventh century," Paul said.

"It's renowned for its chocolates," I remarked, "But the shops will all be shut now so that's no reason to go."

"Have you looked outside Paul? It's much too dark! We wouldn't see anything," John said.

At that remark we gave up all idea of going and went back to our rooms to get an early night.

## Friday August 27th

Treignac to Benevent L'Abbaye
63 miles Grand total 457 miles

Odile served us the standard French breakfast. We were joined by a well-matured French couple, possibly older than us, which gave Paul the chance to try his French. I understood a few words but Ray looked lost. They were on holiday and had driven down from Paris to stop overnight wherever there was a good walk.

Just as we set off Paul said, "I would like to stop at Treignac to take some photographs."

So a few miles on we stopped at a bridge going over a river on the outskirts of Treignac. Paul and I strutted round the main square, with a central water fountain, taking photographs and filming whilst Ray and John waited patiently on their bikes. "Treignac doesn't look very beautiful in this dull weather," I said.

"The river is the Vézère. It attracts many canoeists. In June 2000, Treignac organized the championships of the world for the canoe-kayak descent. Over 40,000 people came to Treignac to watch it—a fantastic number for such a small place," Paul remarked.

I laughed. "You're a store of useless information aren't you Paul."

"I stayed near here in my twenties so I have maintained an interest since."

"A shame there's no shops around here. I fancied buying some of the famous chocolates."

Again the cycling was up and down hills, no sooner reaching the bottom of one hill to then cycle up the next hill. I said to Paul as we were cycling slowly side-by-side at the time, "If only they could install ski lifts to take you up these hills then it would be wonderful".

"Yes but it's a good day for cycling. The sky looks quite blue, there is no wind and it is quite cool."

"I've brought a few bottles of suntan oil and even bought some lip salve just in case. I've not yet had to use either. I'm still sweating a lot though."

"With all these hearty breakfasts, hearty lunches and hearty dinners I am worried that I am putting on weight. I think my belt is getting tighter."

"I'm more worried that I will be an odd shape," I laughed. "All my sweat seems to migrate to my headband!"

Paul cycled alongside Ray and said, "What's your total mileage now? I'm reading 480 miles."

"I'm also reading 480 miles," Ray replied smiling.

"That's odd—you should be at least fifty miles less as you caught the train to Belves."

Ray laughed, "We didn't really catch the train. John's bike had been ready when we arrived at the bike shop, and to catch you up we cycled along the fast straight route, and came very close to meeting you at Monflaquin."

I had been listening to this exchange cycling on their tail. "You don't expect us to believe that do you Ray?" I questioned sceptically. "No sensible person would claim they came by train when they came by bike. The world now believes you came by train."

John came alongside, "There were no trains that ran from Agen to Belves at that time—you can check it out."

"What was the point of the deception then?" asked Paul.

Ray just shrugged and cycled faster closely followed by John.

I began to hear a clicking noise from around my bottom bracket. I was surprised, as it had been replaced as part of the maintenance. I wondered what it could be.

I had always been keen to cycle up to two thirds of the way before stopping for lunch as I felt that I would be able to relax knowing that the second part of the day would be easier. The others liked to stop at about 12:30 each day. On this day I had the map and spied two places where we could stop but when we arrived each one was too small to have any restaurants. I was getting worried as the others had wanted to stop much earlier and I had pushed them on. Finally we found a place to eat after forty-two miles in Bourganeuf, which was just shutting but they agreed to serve us beef burgers. I was saved!

At last we passed the halfway point on the ride Paul and I were walking up a steep hill and were resting our biffons. We shook hands as if we had reached the moon.

We arrived at Benevent L'Abbaye and I think this was the day when I felt the most tired, even though the ride to Auch was tougher. We headed straight to the Chambre D'Hote accommodation La Buissoniere that had been booked by John. He said," It's owned by Alexia Robins and her brother Terry—they are English. She sent me directions. I think we need to turn left then go up a steep hill."

"I hope you are right," I gasped, "I've never felt so knackered."

After a few hundred yards, he exclaimed just outside some gates, "We are here."

I said, "Thank God."

I could see through the gates a large peach-painted house that had a massive garden overlooking distant hills. "This looks wonderful," Paul remarked. "You have done us proud here."

"Look! They've even set up a patio set of chairs and a table under a large gazebo in the back garden," Ray exclaimed.

I thought John had chosen well and began to feel quite kindly towards him. A dog came bounding out to greet us. We walked up the path and out came a man and woman who both looked to be in their early fifties. The woman said, "I am Alexia and this is Terry. Did you have a hard ride?"

"I'm knackered," I replied, with sweat still streaming out of every pore.

"You are lucky you came this year," stated Terry, "you would have melted last year—it was 40 DegC."

Paul laughed, "Probably Mike and I would have left a trail of sweat across the ground like a snail."

"It's been an easy day," said Ray, looking very happy that he could speak and be understood. He had never learnt any French so had not been able to have a conversation with anyone except us lot.

Terry asked, "Would you all like a beer?" and we all nodded in the affirmative. I nodded the most in case I might get two beers—I was feeling parched.

We stood with them in the garden talking and admiring the house. "How long have you been here?" Ray asked now becoming positively talkative.

Alexia replied, "We bought the house fifteen months ago. Initially we spent all our time improving the house, decorating the rooms, fitting new showers and painting the outside. We've now almost finished."

"What made you give up everything in England and move to France?" Paul asked.

Alexis replied, "Our parents died leaving us enough money for the deposit on the house. I had been a health visitor and moved around several places in the southwest of England. I have a son but never married and brought up him by myself. My dream for many years had been to buy a house in France and make my living by turning it into a guesthouse."

Terry came in, "I had lived with my parents all my life, never married, and am a British Olympic team karate coach. I spend half my time in this house in France and the other half sleeping in a caravan parked in a friend's garden in England."

I thought people have strange lives and remarked, "You certainly look like you are enjoying yourself despite all the travelling."

"Have you been accepted as part of the local community?" John asked.

Alexia replied, "The street we are on is known as 'Angleterre Road' as five English couples live on it, however the French were pleased to have us relocate here as we brought income into the village."

Terry explained further, "There are some English enclaves where they have no intention to mix with the French, played cricket, and continuing as if they live in England. The French don't appreciate those kind of settlers or make them welcome."

John said, ever one for statistics, "It is remarkable how many houses in France are now owned by British nationals—over 500,000. I read that by 1997 52,000 Britons had emigrated to France and 47,000 French had emigrated to Britain—I was surprised that the numbers were almost equal."

"Be warned," said Terry smiling, "You might see a few children about. One is my nephew and the other three are in my karate club. I often bring children from my club—they get a holiday and in return they help us with the decorating."

"Sounds like a fair exchange," Paul responded.

"About time we showed you to your rooms," said Terry. "Be careful when you shut the bedroom windows as they have just been painted. We only started to take guests in January and we are just finishing off the paintwork."

We went into the house with most of the downstairs being a fresh-looking open-plan, with a large kitchen area, a long and wide dining-table, and a secluded lounge area with two settees, a deep chair and a large TV. We all disappeared into our bedrooms to clean up and when I came down Alexia was preparing the dinner and Terry was sprawled on the settee watching the Olympic Games. The whole place seemed very homely. Terry remarked, "Paula Radcliffe is running in the marathon at about seven o'clock."

I went outside and photographed Ray sitting at the far end of the garden with the owner's enormous dog being his companion as they both looked across to the distant hills. I saw a washing line outside and asked if I came peg out my washing—I thought if the rain does not stop and the sun shine strongly soon then I will run out of clothes.

Alexia called us to eat and I was a bit disappointed as the four boys were eating with us, which led to the conversation being rather stilted, and Terry checking that the boys were eating their food. From our viewpoint it would have been much better to have just had Alexia and Terry's company as we could have learnt more about this area, however the food was excellent, and we were only charged £10 per head including wine and liqueurs.

Paula Radcliffe's race was on and we all gathered around the TV to watch it—but were disappointed when she lost. "It's getting too late to explore Benevent L'Abbaye—what are we missing Terry?" Paul asked.

"The main attraction is the 12th century Abbey. You could have watched the locals play boule in the Abbey grounds or gone on a pub crawl round the three bars," Terry replied.

"I am almost enticed to jump on my bike but I think I am too tired to cock my leg over the crossbar," I said tiredly.

# The Loire Valley

The valley of the Loire is renowned for its sumptuous chateaux, and is rich both in history and architecture. Orleans was France's intellectual capital in the 13th century, attracting artists, poets and troubadours to the royal court. But the medieval court never stay in one place for long, which led to the building of magnificent chateaux all along the Loire. Chambord and Chenonceau, the two greatest Renaissance chateaux, remain prestigious symbols of royal rule, resplendent amid vast hunting forests and waterways.

This area benefits from temperate climates. Summers are pleasant with maximum temperatures generally 20 to 30 DegC, although it sometimes rises to the mid-thirties, and it is possible to be caught in a sudden downpour.

The Loire Valley had been our two-night stopover point in 1993 on the way to the Dordogne. I do remember seeing some of the chateaux and we joined a guided tour round one though I never understood a word as the guide spoke French very fast all the time.

### Saturday August 28th

Benevent L'Abbaye to Argenton-sur-Creuse
44 miles Grand total 501 miles

I oiled my chain profusely before we set out but I was not hopeful that the oil would solve my clicking problem, as the chain had still looked lubricated.

After yesterday's hard ride I had become accustomed to expecting hills and long slow slogs up them—however the route this day turned out to be the flattest yet. Just after we set out we had a good view of Benevent L'Abbaye, as the house was on a hill above it, and we could see the Abbey below. We passed a cemetery that was similar to other French cemeteries, containing greenhouses around gravestones—why do the French go to these lengths for the dead? Do they grow tomatoes in the greenhouses? But when I looked there were only flowers. I said to Paul who was standing close by, "I remember a tale I was told by a friend years ago. Her grandfather was renowned for having the best tomatoes for miles around. She later learnt that he never went to the toilet in his house but used his own faeces as manure for the tomatoes."

I offered half of a GO energy bar to Paul as we were walking along giving our biffons a rest and he was very pleased since he had become used to just buying bananas and grapes from the shops we passed. I had bought a few of these of various flavours of which my favourite was called 'Cherry and Vanilla'.

"I'm not convinced that these make much of an effect," I remarked, "I've had a few when the going has been tough and I still ended up leading at the back going up hills, and seeing three bikes disappear into the distance."

Paul laughed, "You shouldn't blame these bars for that. Your overall weight of the bike, bags and especially you is too heavy. This one tastes fantastic."

"No need to get personal," I grinned. "Jeff, our self-appointed GASBAGS nutrient advisor, advised to take GO Gell sachets, so I popped into Biketraks and bought a few at £1 each. I ate my last one first thing today."

"Have they made any effect?"

"Up till now I have not noticed any effect. I slipped one in just before lunch one day and noticed that my eating speed improved!" I laughed. "They may have done more good by placing in a plastic bag and using them as more protection for my biffon."

"What made Jeff recommend them?"

"He had been reading an article about them that made great claims. The company that makes them, Science in Sport, claim that they grew out of the desire to provide the best nutritional products and advice to athletes. The Company mixes qualified sport scientists, food technologists, and a physician with keen athletes and sports people who have competed from local level to the world stage. As a result of all this experience they claim they have an unprecedented knowledge of the nutritional needs of athletes. They grew in cycling thanks in part to the use and endorsement of the products by Chris Boardman."

"Best not to argue with the likes of Chris Boardman who is a much better cyclist than you—you aren't even in the same league."

"Yes but I am not sure that Gell tablets are right for long distance touring. I read up about them—it seems that each sachet contains 25g of isotonic carbohydrate energy. That's enough energy for 20 to 30 minutes of exercise, and because it's isotonic, it will still deliver energy without the need for extra water. So on a eight hour trip I would need to take at least sixteen."

"It would be an expensive way to cycle. What does isotonic mean? Is it a word just used to help advertise the tablets?"

"I wondered what the word 'isotonic' meant so I checked my dictionary and it was not listed. Then I found it defined on an Internet Medical dictionary, 'A solution that has the same salt concentration as the normal cells of the body and the blood. An isotonic beverage may be drunk to replace the fluid and minerals which the body uses during physical activity'."

Paul's mind became focussed on phoning Stuart MacFarlane again at Radio Cleveland, and just after the news at eleven we were on and again 'reporting from France'. Stuart McFarlane asked his audience the same as the previous week, "Do you remember the four fifty-year old men cycling across France from Biarritz raising money for charity? Well they are on the phone now."

I could imagine another fifty listeners shaking their heads.

Stuart asked, "Hi Paul, how far have you cycled?"

Paul replied, "We have passed half way."

"How far is that?"

"Over four hundred and fifty miles. We are on our way to Argenton-sur-Creuse."

"Hopefully nothing to do with Cruise missiles," Stuart laughed, "You all must be knackered."

Paul continued, "Certainly sweaty. Just to remind your listeners—We are raising money for MacMillan's Cancer Relief, Alzheimer's Society…"

By this time I was making exasperated mouth movements to convey it was my turn. Paul finally passed over his mobile and I just managed to get in a few words about being one of the other cyclists on the ride. As Paul and I were talking to Stuart, John jumped off his bike and started to run to get rid of his excess energy or was it to ensure he would not be close enough to be heard on the radio? Ray ensured that he was far enough away to not get asked to speak. When we had talked about publicity to both Ray and John during the planning stage, they had been adamant that they would not appear on any radio or TV shows, and were not prepared to take time for photographs which would appear in the press.

The effect of these radio appearances on the sponsorship had not yet been great, in fact it could be called nil, but we felt we must go on trying.

We stopped for lunch and three of us ordered a special type of sausage. The meal arrived with the sausage being served in a white sauce with chips, French beans and spinach. Ray remarked, "The sausage look rather odd," and he started to dissect his. "I'm not eating this—it's revolting—it's guts and intestines."

By this time Paul had eaten half of his but now exclaimed, "I've lost my appetite," and shoved his plate to one side.

"Well I'm eating mine," I responded. "Think of all the starving kids in Africa." I closed my eyes and continued on.

Just as we left the restaurant the rain started again. Paul remarked, "I'm not wearing my super-dooper breathable raincoat. I was just as wet on the inside as on the outside last time," so he continued in his bike top and got wet through.

"I'm going to give my super-dooper breathable raincoat one last chance," I said, but without avail as I still ended up wet through inside.

We passed the 500-mile mark and celebrated in the rain just as we arrived at 'Badecon Le Pin'. John took photographs of Paul in his totally wet light blue short-sleeved shirt, Ray in his yellow raincoat with the hood over his head, me in my blue raincoat, and all wearing shorts. I sent one of the photographs to Naoko.

Her next email said, "I thought you lost weight but you look fatter". When I checked the photograph I realised I had my camcorder bag under my raincoat (my excuse).

I had noticed that the clicking noise on my bike had disappeared indicating that I had had a dry chain link—I realised that I must lubricate my chain more often in future.

We arrived at our hotel two kilometres outside Argentan-sur-Creuse and the rain had stopped. The hotel was alike to a Little Chef with a few bedrooms. I said, "We've arrived quite early for once. Let's get changed and walk into Argenton-sur-Creuse."

I thought, at last, I could look round a town. Just as we set out the rain started again in earnest, and I decided to stop to update the website and watched the other three trudge off in their raincoats and shorts.

I received an email from Jeff, "We beat Crystal Palace today 2-1. Popovic scored an own goal then Hasselbaink nipped in the near the end to score the winner. That gives us seven points out of twelve as last weekend we lost to Arsenal 3-5 and we beat Fulham away mid-week 2-0. Birmingham lost to Spurs 0-1 giving them just four points—tell Paul".

I had a season ticket to watch Middlesbrough and went along with Jeff to every home match. Middlesbrough are in the Premier League and we were hoping for further success this year, after winning the League cup the previous season, as we had just signed Mark Viduka from Leeds and Jimmy Floyd Hasselbaink from Chelsea, two top strikers. However I had noticed previously that top strikers quite often stop 'striking goals' once they were signed by Boro. At least Hasselbaink had now scored two as he had also scored in the opening match against Newcastle, an excellent match that I had watched. Paul supported Birmingham where he had been born, and although he had lived on Teesside for almost twenty years he still supported Birmingham and even is prepared to drive to their ground to watch them—a round trip of almost four hundred miles. It is easy to tell Paul comes from Birmingham as he has a broad Brummie accent. Neither Ray nor John had any interest in football.

Three totally wet beings appeared just past eight o'clock. I said, "I'm glad I didn't go. You look wet through. Did you see much?"

Paul replied, rubbing his hair with his towel, "A fantastic walk. Argenton-sur-Creuse is very attractive even in the rain."

"I agree," said John, dripping on my bed. "We walked up the picturesque street of 'La Coursiere' that led to the top of a hill where the chapel of 'Bonne Dame' stands. From there we overlooked the town and could see beautiful landscapes, steep rocks and green hills along the loops of the river Creuse."

"Many of the houses were medieval and had balconies and red or grey roofs. It's claimed that it has often inspired famous writers," Ray came in, and promptly farted

"Go and do that in your own," I growled. "A shame I didn't go—it sounds like I missed quite an experience. At least Boro won—Jeff sent me an email."

"What about my beloved Birmingham?" Paul asked hopefully.

"They lost 0-1 to Spurs. Now we have seven points to your four. Up the Boro!"

## Sunday August 29th

Argentan-sur-Creuse to Lignieres
52 miles Grand total 553 miles

At last a day arrived when I could expect a relatively flat ride and that is how it turned out. We passed through Argenton-sur-Creuse and I thought it was a rather nondescript place, but it was still damp and the sky grey. I just photographed the war memorial to the children of Aubigny who died between 1939 and 1945.

We arrived in Lignieres and slowly circled round the town to discover that everything was shut. As we passed the town hall John said, "Even this looks shut—you would have thought the mayor would be standing outside to greet us," and he laughed.

"It is Sunday—he would have been otherwise," replied Paul and he grinned.

"And where's the crowd to cheer us in?" laughed Ray.

Finally we found one cafe open where we celebrated our arrival with a beer. "I believe you had difficulty booking the accommodation," I said.

John replied, "I initially tried to book a hotel but had found nothing was available. You saw as we passed the Hotel de France that even that hotel was boarded up So, I contacted the Tourist Office and Marie-Christine came back with just one place where we could stay. It seems that we will be sleeping in a barn close to a former mill and the Arnon River. The toilets are outdoors."

"Doesn't sound too good," said Ray

"Let's hope the barn is not rat infested," I said in a concerned voice.

"I'm worried about my morning constitutional—I don't like outside toilets but this place is all I could get," John said.

"Did you get directions?" asked Paul.

John replied, "Yes—From La Chatre, follow Lignières directions—take the first path on your right just close to the sign post indicating you are in Lignières. Follow the path and the property is on your right—it's at the end of this path."

We went down the path and came to a gate. There were high bushes on the left of a long drive and a massive stone-built barn-type building, easily fifty metres long, on the right. At the end of the drive we could see lawns, with a badminton net erected on it, and in the far distance a forest of trees. "What a wonderful place," remarked Paul.

"There's quite a crowd over there," Ray said, looking towards the barn.

We walked slowly along the path. A casually dressed distinguished-looking man around our age came towards us smiling. "I am Denis Brule and here is my wife Genevieve. We are having a family re-union with all our children and grandchildren." His English was perfect but he spoke with a French accent.

We could see most of them running round a table-tennis table inside the barn. "First meet my father," said Denis. "He normally lives in a nursing home but we brought him out for the day as he enjoys meeting all his family. Unfortunately he has Parkinson's disease and is confined to a wheelchair."

The crowd playing table-tennis then noticed us and came out to greet us. "Meet my three daughters and husbands and boyfriends," said Denis. We all shook hands and introduced ourselves in English.

Denis took us round the back. We looked around astonished at the beautiful setting with a river flowing alongside the main house with a small bridge which looked to lead to what I assumed was the sleeping barn. Denis said, "Have a sit down. You must be tired. Would you all like a beer?"

We all nodded still trying to take in this paradise and the wonderful greeting. I could see a small outhouse building with two brown doors and beyond that a lawn area going along the river bank with a row of tall poplar trees running parallel to the bank. We quenched our thirst with double cans of cold French beer. Denis said, "Come. I will show your sleeping accommodation. Bring your bikes—you can park them in the basement of the barn."

He led us over the bridge and up some steps to the first floor. Wow! What a surprise! The stone-built barn had been totally converted and it must have cost a fortune. It was decked out with pine boarding, with the large area being split by the stairs into the bedroom with six beds and a comfortable lounge. Genieve appeared, "Mike, you must have the double bed. You are so big. I will fetch some more sheets," and disappeared to get bedding.

Denis explained about the outside toilets. "When we bought the property it had two quaint outdoor toilets that you will have passed across the bridge. We decided to keep them. Please can you make sure you flush them by throwing water, in the buckets you will find there, down the hole. If the buckets need refilling you should drop the buckets by a rope into the river."

We threw some of our belongings on the beds then followed Denis back down the stairs and when we reached the bridge he said, "It's quite safe to swim in the river. It is best to enter it over there," and he pointed to where the lawn led gently into the river behind the barn.

Ray, John and myself quickly changed and walked round to the grass verge adjacent to the river whilst Paul stretched himself out on his towel to sunbathe. Ray did his normal back handstand entry into the water, whilst John eased his way in. I crawled on my backside across the stones, touched the cold water and decided that I would prefer to sunbathe.

I returned to find Paul chatting up Agnes, one of the daughters, next to the table-tennis table. I thought that perhaps this was the reason he hadn't been keen to swim!

"I live in Paris with my boyfriend and work for Amnesty International," Agnes said, and continued excitedly, "I am organising a conference in Montreal aimed at getting rid of capital punishment across the world. You should come to it."

I could see Paul starting to wish that he was thirty years younger as he stared into her eyes. I must admit that she was certainly effervescent and enchanting to men of our age.

The elder daughter also lived in Paris with her husband and children and they disappeared to return home after a short time.

The youngest daughter lived in London and had brought across her fairly recently met English boyfriend. She told us about her trip to Peru a few weeks before, which she had booked prior to falling in love. What was remarkable was that everyone could speak very good English. We were to find out why later.

Ray challenged Agnes to a game of table tennis and tried hard to lose. I challenged John to a game and said he could have ten start. He was now very confident but with my past experience I won much to his chagrin. Agnes's boyfriend then thrashed me! Denis and Genieve were now playing boule with their younger daughter and boyfriend—a typical French scene.

My bowels were reaching the point when they had to be released down the outside toilet. I threw water down to flush then walked to the river and dropped in the bucket holding the rope. I pulled and, oh no, the rope came off the bucket. How embarrassing! I stepped over the bridge side and leant over to just reach the bucket. Agnes came up to help, laughing, "Don't worry. It is no problem. It often happens." She certainly had charm—I also began to wish I was thirty years younger.

I heard Ray shout there was an animal caught in a cage down the river. Everyone went along to take a look. It was about the size of a large beaver. "What sort of animal is that?" Ray asked.

"It's a Coypu," Denis replied. "They are South American rodents, and are farmed for their fur."

"What's it doing in France then?" Paul asked inquisitively.

"A few have been imported. They are vegetarians but eat away at the riverbank and cause erosion so we have permission to kill them."

"The poor things has a bloody nose from chewing the cage wire," I remarked.

"Denis will be put it out of its misery now, "Genevieve said and laughed. "It will end up as pate on the table tonight!"

Our vegetarian GASBAGS member Pam would not be happy at this thought. I disappeared fast as I didn't want to watch it being killed.

In the evening Denis and Genevieve cooked us a meal (not Coypu and chips!). Genevieve's sister and husband, the youngest daughter and her English boyfriend joined us. By now Agnes and her boyfriend had left so all flirting by us old men had to stop. I cannot remember much about the French food but I do remember Denis bringing out numerous bottles of wine for us to try—perhaps why I can't remember the food!

We learnt more of Denis's background. He was a journalist and had spent time all over the world. He had spent four years in the USA, two years covering Carter and two years covering Reagan. His family had lived in Washington and he had worked in the White House. When the Presidents had used the Presidential Jets he had gone along. He had also worked in London for a few years, and also had run a team of Far-East correspondents when living in China with numerous trips to other far-east countries including Japan. I proudly told him about my three trips to Japan with ICI and my Japanese girlfriend. During his time in China, Genevieve had learnt Chinese.

John asked, "How were we able to book to stay in this wonderful setting?"

Denis replied, "The Tourist Agency contacted us to see if there was any possibility that we could put you up in our barn. We took pity on you, as we also love cycling and agreed you could stop with us." We are finding that all the French have a very generous spirit.

After the meal we trooped through to the lounge where Denis brought out some liqueurs and we chatted more about his time in the USA. He had thought that Carter had been a very sincere politician at that time (and subsequent events have proved Denis right as Carter has become involved in many good causes). However he did not have much time for Reagan who he considered a well-speaking fool. Denis's views on Iraq mirrored the French government's views on Iraq. The war should not have been started without the backing of the UN. Meanwhile the daughter showed her boyfriend all their photograph albums—love is a wonderful thing.

"Why did you buy this house?" Paul asked, "it is a long way from the main cities."

"We bought it as a retirement home a few years ago," replied Genevieve.

"We set about renovating it straight away. I still work part time as a journalist in Paris but I now enjoy spending my time here after all the years we spent abroad," said Denis.

"We also bought a mansion just up the road 'La maison des Parfums' which we have massively renovated and it is now ready for renting out. It has nine bedrooms and we aim to just rent it out to groups that take over the place for a week or so," continued Genevieve.

Later, whilst I was updating the website, Paul, Ray and John were shown round 'La maison des Parfums' and were mightily impressed. Would this be suitable for a GASBAGS major ride?

Denis remarked, "There is some wonderful countryside around Lignieres and there are some fabulous cycling rides. The countryside is a landscape of well-kept family farms and meadows neatly bordered by hedgerows. I like to take out our grandchildren on bike rides. I am thinking of preparing a guide to good cycling rides."

"What's the history of Lignieres," I asked.

Denis replied, "It was the centre of Calvinism when the famous protestant reformer was a student at Bourges."

"Have you ever been involved in the twinning association? I believe Lignieres is twinned to Dunbar on the east coast of Scotland, about 60 miles from Edinburgh," Paul asked.

"Not personally," Denis replied. "I know about the background though. After the Lignieres college principal's stay in Dunbar back in the 1980's, a regular correspondence began between the college of Lignieres and the Dunbar Grammar School. The first school exchange took place in 1990. Dunbar took the first step to show its desire to set up a twinning agreement between the two cities. In September 1992, a French delegation went to Dunbar to create the first official links. In May 1993, it was the turn of Dunbar."

"Do you know if there have been many exchanges? Great Ayton is twinned with Ouzouer and there are regular exchanges," I said.

"There have been several trips that have enabled the French to discover Scotland and vice versa. The Scottish choir came to the Cathedral of Bourges, the church of Chezal-Benoit and Lignieres to give a concert. Famous musicians went to Dunbar to play in concerts as well. Both Scottish and French people take part in all the events that can reinforce these links," replied Genevieve.

"Do you know why Lignieres is twinned with a place as far away as Dunbar? It must be over 800 miles away," said Ray, for once taking an interest in twinning—probably picturing the route in his mind due to his Ordnance survey job.

"I think it is to do with the 'Auld Alliance'. Do you know much about it?" asked Denis. We all shook our heads. He continued, "It was first agreed in the late thirteenth century and was built on Scotland and France's shared need to curtail English expansion. Primarily it was a military and diplomatic alliance but for most of the population it brought tangible benefits through pay as mercenaries in France's armies and the pick of the finest French wines."

"I like French wines so it seems a good alliance to me," John laughed.

"Dunbar was the one place that advertised our ride," I remarked. "We based this ride upon cycling through twinned towns of which we found sixteen. Paul first wrote to all the mayors of all the French twinned towns, and then I sent an email to all the mayors of all the English towns that they were twinned with. We hoped that the all the twinned towns would combine and help us raise sponsorship. For Dunbar I sent the email to the their website contact."

"Did you get much response?" asked Genevieve.

"Approximately nil," laughed Ray.

"They are all probably biding their time to meet us at Caen," said Paul smiling.

That night I laid my torch next to my pillow as I assumed I would awake in the dark and have the need to go to the outdoor toilets. I was right. I awoke in the dark, turned on my torch and tiptoed downstairs. I saw the outdoor toilets some way off not looking very inviting. I thought what the hell and had my tinkle over the bridge into the river. I thought that should give the coypu a new refreshing taste!

## Monday August 30th

Lignieres to Aubigny sur Nère
66 miles Grand total 619 miles

Denis and Genevieve prepared a typical French breakfast. They showed us the brochures that they had prepared in both English and French for their rental property 'La maison des Parfums'.

"We have a website for the place on www.maisondesparfums.com. We have commissioned that the brochure be translated into Japanese as well," said Denis.

"I'm surprised that the Japanese want to come so far south of Paris," I said. "It must be almost 200 miles south."

"They like the tranquillity and peacefulness of the countryside down here," replied Genevieve.

"It has now been weeks since we commissioned the Japanese brochure," said Denis.

"I could ask my Japanese partner, Naoko, to translate it if you like?" I responded.

"That's a good idea. Give her my email address please."

We were wondering about the bill after having accommodation, dinner, breakfast, beer, wine, and liqueurs. The bill turned out to be just £17 each so we each left a tip, which in no way could compensate for the wonderful welcome we had received and being made to feel so at home.

Before we left Denis brought out his new expensive racing bike that he had been bought as a gift by a colleague as thanks to starting him off in a career in journalism. Ray, our biking expert, became very animated and bent down to examine the gears and the brakes. He enthused about the bike's pedigree and was glad that for once he was understood in France.

Denis and Genevieve waved us goodbye. As we cycled along the path leaving the house John said, "I would like to call in at the Tourist Office to thank Marie-Christine for all her time and effort in booking this place." We all agreed he should.

We parked up outside the Tourist Office and John went in. I put my head round the door and heard John ask, "Is Marie-Christine here? I am John—you booked us in at Denis and Genevieve's barn."

A very attractive young lady said, "I am Marie-Christine. Can I help?"

I am sure that John began to play up to her. "I have come to thank you for such wonderful accommodation," he said in a manner of a couple having their first date. I realised I was not welcome and backed out of the door.

As we cycled out of town Ray shouted to me, "What's that brown mark on your cycling shorts?"

I had attached all my wet clothes that I had hurriedly washed the previous evening to my top rear bag and my cycling shorts were on display to the world inside out. John laughed, "It's a skid mark!"

Paul cried, "Hide them quickly—the world doesn't want to see that." Feeling rather embarrassed I stashed them in my bag.

We had travelled about four miles with me being about twenty yards behind the other three when a car shot past me, braked and stopped on the verge. Out jumped Genevieve, "I found these socks and underpants in the barn. Whose are they?"

By this time the other three had come back. "They are mine. Thanks for bringing them. I've never been chased before by such a sophisticated lady," Paul laughed. I felt like asking Genevieve if there were any skid marks on his pants but thought the better of it—she looked too refined to even know what skid marks were!

After Genevieve had left, Paul began to tell tales about some of his past girlfriends that had chucked him out of their houses, and thrown his smalls after him—not a small list!

As we passed through Bourges I spied an ATM and Paul, Ray and I withdrew money as we were becoming short. I had only taken £500 converted into Euros as I had realised that I would be able to pay most Hotel bills with VISA and I knew I would be able to withdraw any more money required from a cash machine using my Switch card. Both Paul and Ray also had Switch cards. "Do you want some money John?" I asked.

John replied, "I never withdraw money from a cash machine and I decided that I was not going to change my practice for this trip. I brought £1,000 converted to Euros instead."

"You are an accountant, aren't you John" stated Paul. "About time you came into the real world."

"Not for much longer," replied John. "Once I retire early next year I intend to never work as an accountant again. Perhaps I will help out with gardens."

"You're too young to retire," I declared.

"I'm not," said John. "I'm been planning for retirement at fifty for years. I have quite enough savings."

Ray laughed. "I've heard that the Queen blinks when you take out a twenty pound note."

"It's about time the UK decided to switch to the Euro," I declared, to switch the subject, "it would make life much easier."

"I agree," said Paul. "Money is just a way of facilitating the transfer of goods, and as we now do most of our trade with the European Union it would be eminently sensible to switch to the common currency, which is now in use in Belgium, Germany, Greece, Spain, France, Ireland, Italy, Luxembourg, the Netherlands, Austria and Finland."

"Don't forget Portugal as well. I've booked to go there next year," piped up Ray.

"The only legitimate argument, in my view, against switching is that we want to have control of our own interest rates. However the dollar is in use across the USA and has been able to overcome such a problem. The population of the European Union at 450 million shouldn't make much difference compared to the 280 million in the US," I argued.

"A major benefit I've read is the shelter from external shocks. The euro area is far better equipped than the previous national currencies to withstand external economic shocks or fluctuations in the external exchange rate vis-à-vis the US dollar and other major currencies", Paul said.

"I'm against switching," John said. "I prefer to be a little Englander."

"You're small enough," I laughed.

"This is our seventh twinned town," Paul remarked. "It's twinned with Peterborough."

Ray smirked. "So that's seven twinned towns where we haven't yet met a mayor."

We climbed back on our bikes and carried on with the ride after this diversion. The ride was almost uneventful as the route was for once very flat and we covered the ground fairly fast, arriving in Aubigny sur Nère by four thirty. We cycled slowly along the main street admiring its 15th and 16th century half-timbered houses and colourful flower arrangements. "It looks very picturesque. It looks to be a bit bigger than Stokesley," John remarked.

"I checked out this town," I said. "The population is around 6,000. Let's ask at the Tourist Office how to get to the hotel."

"I'm not going near there," said John. "It's very close to the Town Hall and I don't want to be attacked by the mayor—he might recognise your GASBAGS shirt Mike."

"Nor me," said Ray, backing up his room partner.

After getting directions we cycled up to the hotel. There was a notice stating that booking in started at five o'clock so we sat outside in the sunshine. A woman arrived at ten to five, unlocked the door, and went in. I followed her and was told in no uncertain terms to get out and wait till five o'clock. I thought very customer friendly!

In the evening we assumed that there would be street restaurants as we had found further south in France and were disappointed to find there were none; in fact the nightlife was approximately nil. We ate in an upmarket expensive restaurant though the food was not very appetising. To pass the time I asked Paul, "Do you know the history of this town?" not really expecting he would but he came up with the goods.

"We were told about the history of this town when I visited Ouzouer as it is very interesting. In the early fifteenth century, during the Hundred Years War, when the English possessed more than half of France, the future King Charles VII of France, hemmed in by the English, near Bourges, invoked the Auld Alliance with the Scots. He appealed for help to the Regent of Scotland who sent across a large army under the leadership of Sir John Stuart. The Scots contributed greatly to the defeat of the English, although they themselves suffered heavy casualties. A year later, as a reward for their brilliant service, Sir John Stuart and his successors were given the possession of Aubigny and the surrounding lands."

"You do have a good memory," remarked John.

"I've always taken an interest in history," Paul continued, "for more than 200 years, succeeding Stuarts continued to give outstanding service to Aubigny-sur-Nere—City of the Stuarts. It was only in the early nineteenth century that the town became French again due to the desultory interest of the Scottish and the upheavals of the French Revolution."

"This town is twinned to Haddington in East Lothian, almost 800 miles away—perhaps again due to the Auld Alliance," I remarked. "I actually found a website written by Haddington dedicated to their twinned town but I couldn't find any evidence of cultural exchanges."

After the meal we tried to find a downmarket pub, but found none so went back to the hotel where we were refused a drink unless we drank outside and by now the temperature was quite low. Perhaps the hotel was upset that we hadn't eaten there. We had an early night for once.

I checked my emails when I returned to my room and I had one from Paul Mckintosh:

"Hi Mike,

The diary is superb, very well written, so good in fact, I almost feel as though I am there with you guys. I feel quite envious, whilst some of the days sound as though they have been quite tough in cycling terms, the overall achievement must give you all a terrific feeling of satisfaction in terms of 'your personal challenge' and hopefully a successful fund raising. Paul"

I must admit that I felt rather pleased about Paul's email. I had been writing the diary of the ride for the last ten days and Paul's note made the work all seem worthwhile. I was also pleased that the note had come from Paul whom I had a great deal of respect for. "I've just received an email from Paul Mckintosh," I said to Paul.

"Isn't he the one who organises the annual 30-mile Safeway rides that raises money for charity?"

"Yes—it's now being running for seven years. He's been very brave in switching charities each year. It has raised money for Chloe Brown—she had a rare form of cancer, RVI Newcastle Cancer Unit, Butterwick Hospice, South Cleveland Heart Unit, Multiple Sclerosis, Zoe's Place for Special Neonatal Baby Unit in James Cook University Hospital, and the Motor Neurone Disease Association."

"It is unusual to switch each year. Do you know how much he has raised?"

"In total about £60,000 and on the last ride around 170 riders took part."

"It just shows what personal initiative can achieve."

"I've taken part in them all."

John walked into our room at this point. "I heard you talking about the Safeway ride. I've never taken part. Where does it go?"

"The ride takes in many of the wonderfully scenic parts of what GASBAGS calls 'GASBAGS Land'."

"I'm not a GASBAG don't forget," John grinned.

I continued, "The ride starts in Stokesley, and then goes along the River Leven through Great Ayton and Ingleby Greenhow then up to Clay Bank car park. I once fell off going up to Clay Bank and landed in nettles when I could not extract my feet fast enough from my bike pedal grips much to the amusement of the cyclists going past. The ride continues down to Great Broughton and passes through Kirby, Carlton, Faceby, Potto, Hutton Rudby and finally returns to Stokesley. There are stops at ten mile intervals where there are endless drinks, and oranges, bananas, crisps and chocolates to consume."

"I might take part next year when I will be retired," responded John.

"What I like about the route besides the scenic views," said Paul, "is all the delightful North Yorkshire pubs on the way that serve real beer."

"Great pubs," I said, "I can think of them all now: The Buck Hotel in Great Ayton; The Dudley Arms at Ingleby Greenhow; the Jet Miners at Great Broughton; the Black Swann at Kirby; the Blackwell Ox at Carlton; The Dog & Gun Inn at Potto; The Wheatsheaf Inn at Hutton Rudby; The Kings Head at Seamer; the New Inn at Stokesley. Each pub has its own uniqueness but my two favourites are the Blackwell Ox that serves delicious Thai food and always has on two different real beers, and the White Swann that brews its own real beer and serves a Ploughmans lunch with two types of cheese."

"You should join us John," Paul chuckled.

"You would enjoy Christmas Eve. GASBAGS meets at my house for mulled wine then we cycle the ten miles to the

Blackwell Ox where we book out the front room. Last year, being our first year with real bike shirts, was very special as twenty-two of us cycled along in our matching tops."

"You won't get me in a GASBAGS top," responded John, "I'm an individual."

"Don't forget you said you would if we meet a mayor," I responded.

"There's not much hope of that now," John laughed.

"You're mistaken John," said Paul, "we will meet one tomorrow in Ouzouer."

"At last we will meet your friends Didier and Jocelyn. How did you get to know them?"

"It was through the Great Ayton Twinning Association of course. We joined it at its inception about ten years ago. I took a very active part in helping the association get started. We regularly went on the coach trips to Ouzouer and stayed with Didier and Jocelyn each time—we both had families about the same age. Neither of them can speak much English, so my wife and I had good practice at speaking French."

"I'm glad they agreed to put us all up for two nights. It gives us the chance to have a rest and look around Ouzouer—I have been keen to see Great Ayton's twinned town. I had begun to get worried that their enthusiasm for letting us stay was as not as great as your enthusiasm for stopping there."

"I had begun to get worried," Paul said, "as I sent them an email then didn't get a reply after several weeks. It seems that their PC had not been working. Once I phoned them they said they were very happy for us to stay."

"So what welcome can we expect when we reach Ouzouer? The only welcomes we had up to now were in the two Tourist Offices with Maite at St Palais and Marie-Christine at Lignieres—and we had to go in search of those welcomes!"

"Didier is driving out to meet us at Sully, and a lone cyclist, as a representative of all French cyclists he says, will also come out from Ouzouer to meet us. Didier has offered to take our baggage the last few miles to Ouzouer but I said we were too proud for that and we wanted to complete this magnificent journey with the full kit on-board."

"What about when we leave after our day's rest?"

"We will be accompanied by several cyclists who have decided to take the day off."

"I really am hoping we will be meeting our first mayor."

"Well I wrote to all the mayors of the twinned towns—I have been disappointed up to now but tomorrow should be different. However I am a bit concerned in case the chairman of the Great Ayton Twinning Association has been in touch to say we are not an official visit."

"I can't believe that would happen. Any contact between the English and French must be welcomed I would have thought."

I checked my email after this conversation and I had one from Naoko saying that she was in the middle of a typhoon and her words gave the impression of personal worry. I said to Paul, "I'm worried about Naoko and her two daughters. Japan is being hit by a typhoon. Their island of Kyushu, which is the most southerly of the main four Japanese islands, is where the worst impact of the typhoon is expected to be felt—they can cause immense devastation."

"What exactly is a typhoon?" Paul asked.

"I read up about them as I knew that Japan has quite a few—this year there had been the most in living memory. A typhoon is a strong tropical cyclone, a storm that forms over a body of water and is accompanied by powerful winds and heavy rain. It is the same thing as a hurricane, but 'typhoon' is the name used for storms in the western Pacific Ocean. A 'super typhoon' is a typhoon with winds that blow faster than 150 miles per hour. This one has been given the name Chaba."

## Tuesday August 31st

Aubigny to Ouzouer-sur-Loire
46 miles Grand total 665 miles

Perhaps I was excited about arriving at Ouzouer where we would have a rest day or concerned about Naoko but I woke early then thought I would check my email and add more to the website but when I put on the light at six thirty a voice from the next bed said, "What time do you call this?" so I gave up for a time.

At a more reasonable time I checked my email, as I wanted to check Naoko had survived the typhoon. She had sent me an email, "We are ok but the winds are still quite strong. My aerial has blown off my house. There have been five killed and sixty-one injured in Kyushu."

I felt relieved that she was safe. Both her emails and my emails were always in English as I had tried to learn some Japanese but as yet had only learnt a few words—I enjoy saying 'Konnichiwa' which means Good Afternoon. Naoko's English was excellent, and she knew words that I never knew existed, so was quite happy that we communicated in English. We had met on a dating site on the Internet in January 2003. For nine weeks we communicated daily just by email and then Naoko flew to England when we first talked—a very romantic meeting at Heathrow airport.

Ray and Paul turned up at breakfast in their GASBAGS shirts as we were cycling to Great Ayton's twinned town. "How about wearing my spare GASBAGS shirt John?" I asked.

"I only agreed to wear a GASBAGS shirt if we were going to meet a mayor—and there seems to be little danger of that," replied John.

Paul's mobile rang and he went into conversation for a time speaking in broken French. "That was Didier. Just he will be meeting us at Sully now—the cyclist couldn't get the day off."

"Our welcoming party is getting less and less," I remarked.

"Yes—I think there is a good chance that the Ouzouer twinning association wants this to be seen as a personal visit and not one that's part of the Twinning Association," Paul replied.

"What time are we meeting?" John asked.

"He says he will be at the Sully Chateau at mid-day—he sent his best regards to the indefatigable quartet," Paul replied.

"It's lucky that he can just take an afternoon off—what's his job?" asked Ray.

"He's responsible for security at the Ouzouer Nuclear Power Station. He can be flexible in the times he works," Paul replied.

The route was fairly flat and by ten thirty we arrived at a bridge decked with flowers going over the River Loire. "I wish they would deck our bridges with flowers like this," remarked John, "Perhaps I could become a bridge flower decker when I retire," he laughed.

"Fantastic view down the river, I said, "the ten arch bridge is very attractive."

"That's Gien on the hill beyond the bridge. The plumes of steam are ascending out of the Ouzouer nuclear power station where Didier works," Paul remarked. "I hoped we would have time to look around Gien on the way but we would be late. We will make a very brief stop then carry on to Sully."

"Why didn't we arrange to meet Didier at Gien—it's only six miles from Ouzouer? Going via Sully is eighteen miles—we have to double back on ourselves," I asked plaintively.

"I thought the ride would be too short if we did that," Paul replied, "and there are some very scenic views between Gien and Sully as we cycle along the side of the River Loire."

As we cycled along towards Sully I complained to Paul, "The scenic view is hidden by more sweetcorn fields—they have been non-stop for the past six miles. It makes you wonder if there is a sweetcorn mountain somewhere like the renowned butter mountain."

John overheard my comment and joined us. He shouted to me, "Sweetcorn is the seed of maize. After wheat and rice, maize is the third most frequently cultivated crop worldwide. Maize was indigenous to the Americas and once discovered was rapidly adopted in Europe, Africa and Asia. Its use is dominated by the demand for animal feed. It is also processed into valuable industrial and food products such as ethyl alcohol, maize meal, starch and sweeteners."

"Well we've certainly seen enough of it," I said.

"Yes but Europe still imports an enormous amount from the US," replied John.

We arrived spot-on mid-day at Sully and we parked up adjacent to the Chateau of Sully-sur-Loire, with its four high towers and deep moat. "The chateau is magnificent. Do you know the history of it Paul?" I asked.

"We went round it once when we visited Ouzouer. Inside there are all sorts of tapestries, paintings, sculptures, parts of furniture and architectural curiosities. The most famous of the Chateau's owners was Maximilien de Béthune back in the seventeenth century. He was the first duke of Sully and Grand Minister for the king Henri IV. I believe he created the adjacent park, increased and restored the fortress to its original size, and reinforced the dams to protect the city from raw sewage from the river. During four centuries, the castle remained in the family of the descendants of Sully. In the early sixties it was classified as an historic building and became the property of the Department of Loiret."

Didier was delayed but when he arrived he genuinely seemed pleased to meet us all. He looked to be mid-forties, and was about John's height and build—quite slim. He had short curly dark hair greying at the edges, smiled easily, and was dressed casually in light blue jeans and an open-necked grey shirt.

He brought a cool box out of his car from which he extracted the best raspberry and cream cake I had ever seen and a bottle of peach champagne which he cracked open to celebrate our arrival. I photographed him just as the cork shot in the air and his eyes gave a picture of wide-eyed surprise.

Now was the time to eat to celebrate our arrival, and we sat down in an outdoor restaurant facing the elegant chateau. For a rare time we drank wine over lunch. I soon found that my French was inadequate to converse with Didier whose English was equally poor. So I talked to him through Paul. "Sully is our eighth twinned town on our route. It is twinned with Bradford-on-Avon in Wiltshire and I have found a reference to the President of the Bradford-on-Avon Twinning Association on the Sully website. Do you know if there is any activity between the towns?"

"Yes," Didier replied, "Friends of mine have taken part in quite a few events—they thought Bradford-on-Avon was very picturesque."

We cycled to Ouzouer with Didier in his car behind us, but when we reached the Ouzouer main street he overtook us and drove slowly in front with all his lights flashing like a cavalcade. However no-one seemed to notice us which was rather disappointing. "So, where's the mayor?" laughed John. "You two were so confident last night."

"He's probably tied up in official business," Paul responded, "We're probably pencilled in for tomorrow—we do have a full free day."

"Who are you trying to kid," Ray smirked.

"Just you wait and see," I responded.

Didier & Jocelyne's house turned out to be an exceptionally big bungalow with a large garden growing tomatoes, raspberries, rhubarb, peas, strawberries, beans, cabbages, onions and numerous other types of vegetables. Didier's hobby is to carve in stone and I had my bedroom in the dining room next to a stone fireplace that he had carved. Ray and John were given a room with twin beds but one shared mattress. Ray whispered to Paul, "I can't sleep there—I'm not bloody gay you know."

"It's only for two nights," whispered Paul.

"I'm not being that close to his flatulence," whispered John.

So Paul asked Jocelyne if she could find a way to separate the beds, which she did. Jocelyne then asked us if we would like our clothes washing—we jumped at the opportunity to have them washed in a real washing machine.

Up to now I have not mentioned how proficient we were at French. Paul's French is very good as he had spent five months in France when he was twenty-one. John and I could understand quite a bit of what was being said but had more difficulty in creating sentences. Ray had never learnt French so found it more impossible to get involved when French was the main language spoken. Didier and Jocelyne's English was about as good as my French so most of the conversation was in French with Paul and Didier leading the talking.

Didier and Jocelyne prepared us an excellent meal with cold pork slices, black pudding type sausage, pate, lettuce, hot green beans, crisps followed by a selection of cheeses followed by plum tart and accompanied by as much wine as we could drink. What hospitality—the French know how to entertain.

We were introduced to their daughter Amelie who was seventeen and was about to go to a school in Orleans where she would board four nights a week. Paul had known Amelie for many years and learnt from her that this move to Orleans would be the first time that she had spent time away from home, and she was very apprehensive about starting her new life. I would think that the last thing that she wanted was four cyclists staying in her house! Amelie had a brother Fabien who had now left home but Paul had a good conversation with him on the phone in stilted French.

### Wed September 1st

Ouzouer-sur-Loire
0 miles Grand total 665 miles

Our rest day arrived and we all slept in for a time. I awoke wondering if we really would meet the Mayor of Ouzouer today.

Whilst Didier and Jocelyne prepared us a French breakfast, I checked my email by connecting to their phone line—I politely asked first if they minded and tried to explain that there would only be a local phone connection charge. I had one email from a friend Dave Taylor who lived close by and who I had asked to check my house in Great Ayton every so often. "I found a brand new Fiat car parked outside your house and knowing that you are a highly-paid consultant thought that you had treated yourself. However when collecting your email I found car keys and a note from Eurocar saying that they had delivered the car to the wrong house. They have now been to collect it."

Putting keys in the wrong door seems to be a common problem with car hire companies as it had happened before. I wonder whom they employ to deliver the cars? I was fortunate to have Dave living close by as I could rely upon him to help when needed. I had shared a car club with Dave for many years when we both worked at ICI, and now he had retired and had joined the ICI-retiree dog walkers club. I was determined to not join this fictitious club—many people used to retire young (fifty plus) from ICI and quite a few on my estate. Within days they could be seen walking a dog. I had also retired young at the age of fifty but for five years I had maintained contract work (Dave's definition of highly-paid consultant not being accurate!), and I did not want to become a dog walker yet.

This was the first time I had eaten a breakfast in a French household. They had cereals, which I found surprising, or were they just catering for our English appetite.

"I found it hard to believe the rumour that the Great Ayton Twinning Association may have contacted the Ouzouer Twinning Association to say that we weren't officially representing them," I remarked to Paul.

"I also doubt it," he replied, "it would be small minded if they had done."

"I agree—I would think any contacts between the English and French would be welcome."

"I was involved with the twinning when it first started—I would hope they remember that."

"The contacts between Great Ayton and Ouzouer twinning associations seem to be excellent. I've been involved in a few events when the French visited Great Ayton. I've been to several Ceilidh dances specially arranged for them—they may have begun to assume that us English only like Ceilidh dances," I laughed.

"I enjoy those dances," Didier smiled, "switching partners and dancing with lots of beautiful English women."

"I've been on several of the Great Ayton trips to Ouzouer. The coach trip takes fifteen hours including the time spent on the ferry between Dover to Calais but it is worth it. We have always stopped with Didier and Jocelyne," Paul said, smiling at them both. "Their hospitality has always been fantastic. The entertainment provided by the Ouzouer Twinning Association is excellent. There is normally a folk dance where everyone gets dressed in fancy dress, and with plenty of free flowing wine. We have also been on several canal cruises."

"I enjoyed the time that you, me and Ray cycled to Beverley to meet the French coach that had driven across from the Hull ferry. Us three raced the five Ouzouer cyclists and I was in the lead until we reached a hill. Then I almost stopped and they continued on as if the hill didn't exist."

"Yes—they were remarkably fit. They had cycled all the way from Ouzouer to Zeebrugge—over three hundred miles by then."

"I enjoyed the picnic when the coach stopped on the way back. All the sandwiches, cakes and wine."

"I had tried to get some money to pay for lunch for them but the only money available to the Great Ayton Twinning Association was what is raised from members, whilst the Ouzouer Twinning Association gets subsidised by the town."

"How big is Ouzouer, Didier?" I asked.

"It's less than half the size of Great Ayton—about 2,500 but the surrounding villages get involved in the twinning association as well. Until recently Ouzouer was even smaller but more than doubled in size in the 1970's with the construction of the nuclear power station where I work. There were some complaints when families moved into the village from other parts of France, and many new houses were built. But this influx of newcomers revitalised village life."

"So was it this revitalisation that led to the interest in twinning?"

"Yes—we began to search for a partner in 1995 and the twinning with Great Ayton was agreed in 1997."

Our breakfast finished and I wandered into the garden. Didier was setting up a barbecue. Paul remarked, "It is the usual hospitality. I still can't get over it. Still can't get used to the way that you get looked after here in France. Didier is already preparing for lunch. Barbecue le midi."

Didier walked past saying "Le midi ou le soir?"

"Le midi," Paul replied.

Didier took us for a drive around and within a few hundred yards of his gates we were driving in the immense Orleans Forest that stretches from Ouzouer all the way to Orleans, over 30 miles. We stopped by a lake and went for a walk in the forest. "I hope I don't lose sight of Didier—I can imagine being lost in this forest for a long time," I remarked, "What is he searching for?"

"Edible mushrooms," Paul replied.

"There are edible mushrooms in the forest and ones that can make you violently sick. There are even some that are deadly," Didier continued, overhearing our conversation. "Hunting is not a hobby for the careless or uninformed. Fortunately there are a number of good edible mushrooms that are easy to recognize and hard to confuse with anything dangerously poisonous."

We drove on and stopped in a large clearing with a large War Memorial, one group of nine gravestones and a second group of over sixty gravestones. Didier explained, "This forest was used extensively by the French Resistance, called the Maquis, during the last war, and quite a few died. There is a special story associated with the nine gravestones that I will tell you over lunch."

Next we drove to Lorres to view a 12th century market square building. The roads in Lorres had lampposts with bunches of pink and white flowers in a very healthy state. We drove back through Ouzouer. It seemed to be almost a perfect place to live with big houses and large gardens, and weather that we can only dream of on Teesside. "You are lucky to live here Didier," remarked Paul.

"I agree. I would almost move here but you have no 'Boro'," I laughed. "We are lying fifth in the Premiership, just one place behind Manchester United, and way above Birmingham!"

"There are some people who are unhappy about having a nuclear power station on our doorstep which you don't have," Didier replied.

"We have one that is close enough—at Hartlepool, and it has had a few problems," Ray declared.

"I've enjoyed my visits to Great Ayton. I have enjoyed strolling along the river," Didier said.

"It is quite a tourist resort. On a warm day tourists flock out of Middlesbrough and lie on the Low Green and paddle and fish in the Leven. When I drive home from work with the sun shining on Roseberry Topping, I believe I am living in the best little village in England," I responded.

Back at our 'home', Didier prepared a barbecue outdoors, whilst us four sat in the shade just in shorts. Out came the wine again and we all indulged, except for Didier, as he was intent to drive us on a further exploration after lunch. He asked how we liked our beef. I said well done and Ray said raw. Well Ray's came almost dripping with blood and mine was still red inside. Whilst we were eating Didier and Jocelyne's two dogs were fighting. One was a large black-haired dog and the other was a minute Yorkshire Terrier that I could pick up with one hand. This little dog could be very fierce with the much larger dog, and the two had to be separated to save the big dog's life. It was like David and Goliath.

"So how about telling us about the nine gravestones?" I asked.

"That is quite a tale and well known in Ouzouer," said Jocelyne.

"It is even told at school. It goes by the title 'The Dead Yank Hero of Orleans Forest," said Amelie.

Didier took up the story, "A World War II fighter pilot, listed as killed in action on August 10th, 1944, actually died four days later with the maquis. The row of nine simple wooden crosses marks the spot where he enjoyed his last moment of peace on earth. Just as the crosses were being driven into the ground, a series of shots shattered the dawn quiet of the forest and minutes later, Captain Edward Simpson was dead."

"But he died a hero," continued Jocelyne, "sacrificing his life that a group of freedom fighters he had known only a few days might live. It was August 14th, 1944, the day remembered by the people around this part of France as the 'day that the maquis were attacked'. Members of the maquis who were in the forest that day remember that Simpson joined them late in the evening of August 10th, after his fighter plane was shot down south of the Loire River and several miles from the maquis' forest hiding place. Just after landing, Simpson was contacted by two of the freedom fighters who were returning from carrying messages to the commander of the maquis in four districts of France, who was then near Orleans. The couriers led him back through the German lines to their hiding place. They thought he was British, since the only other English-speaking persons they had met during the war were a few British agents who worked with them."

Didier went on, "At the time Simpson joined the marquis, the Allied forces had pushed to within a few miles of Orleans, and the German troops in the area were showing signs of a retreat to the north. The Free French fighters who had been operating from the Orleans forest for several months were awaiting orders to break out of the woods and join other maquis units in the push to Paris. Rather than run the risk of trying to slip Simpson back to American forces, the maquis leaders suggested to him that he remain with them until it was time for the whole unit to break through the German Panzer division surrounding the forest.

The funeral service Simpson was attending when the attack began was for nine members of the maquis who had been killed in a fire-fight on the outskirts of the forest. Although several of the freedom fighters fell when the patrol opened fire, the well-armed group quickly overpowered the Germans and drove them off. But knowing that their hiding place had been discovered, the Free French—numbering between 200 and 300—decided the time had come to escape from the woods and join the Allied forces near Orleans. Hurriedly breaking camp they had occupied for several months, the hunted men rushed through the woods to their well-hidden motor pool nearly a mile away. Most of their vehicles were captured from the Germans. Simpson found a place on the last truck of the convoy as it broke from cover and raced down one of the forest's narrow trails leading to the Orleans highway. As the maquis vehicles turned on to the highway, they were spotted by a German column of trucks and armoured cars. The Germans pursued the maquis convoy and were rapidly closing in, when Simpson made a decision—and died. Knowing that the German column had to be stopped, one of the Frenchmen riding in the truck with Simpson called for the driver to slow down, and reached for a heavy machine gun. As the truck slowed, Simpson and five of the Frenchmen dropped from it and set up the machine gun in the centre of the road as the truck roared away. All six of the men surely realized that they could not escape death, since the point where they established their roadblock was flat and completely without protective cover. The final action those men fought was brief, but successful. Their first burst of machine-gun fire stopped the lead German vehicle and blocked the road. The Germans kept firing until all six were dead. But the time they gained was enough, for by the time the road was cleared, the maquis convoy was well on the way to Orleans and out of reach of the Germans. The maquis were very impressed with the fact that Simpson gave his life for them even though he didn't have to, and didn't even know those he died with."

"He was a real hero," said Paul, switching from translating.

"Yes," said Jocelyne, "the people of Ouzouer were so impressed that they collected enough money to build a small monument at the scene of the roadblock. Many of our villagers were members of the maquis during the war. The monument lists the names of the six men killed there. Simpson's name also appears on the large monument dedicated to all of the maquis. This second memorial located on a circle in the centre of the forest, is inscribed with the names of those who lost their lives during the bitter fighting in the wood in August 1944."

"What's odd," said Amelie and laughed, "is that Simpson is still listed in the US, it is claimed, as having died on August 10th as the person who buried him couldn't speak English and the Americans who came to collect his body couldn't speak French."

Didier drove us on another whirlwind tour of other places near Ouzouer with French music playing in the car. I had forgotten by this time that we were on a bike ride across France. First we went to Gien and drove alongside the Loire fenced in with a long metal fence with a bunch of flowers at every stanchion. There is no doubt the French like flowers. We parked up at the castle and went for a walk around Gien.

"There are enough shops with tableware," I remarked to Paul.

"Gien is renowned for the fabulous collection of Gien tableware with beautiful patterns and vibrant colours which is known all over the world. We visited here on one of our trips to Ouzouer and I was very impressed," Paul responded.

"The Faienceries de Gien was founded in 1821 in by an Englishman," Didier explained. "Production first began with functional tableware, and then went on to make fancier dinnerware, decorative pieces and fine tableware emblazoned with notable families' coats of arms.

Gien was also famous in the Second World War. On June 11th 1940 German or Italian planes bombarded the small city, and transformed it at once into a significant blazing inferno. The castle was destroyed, and the city was totally disfigured. The rebuilding started in June 1946, dictated by a preoccupation with fidelity—some people say it is the jewel of the French rebuilding."

When we walked back to the car I looked at the castle in a different light now knowing it had been totally rebuilt. I particularly liked the intricate-patterned brickwork alike to what that might be found on crockery.

As we climbed back in the car John started laughing. "That's another twinned town where our welcome by the mayor has been missing."

"You're right—it is twinned to Malmesbury, probably a good match as that town is perched on a hill as well," Paul replied, not taking the bait.

"I don't think it's funny," I said. "Paul and I spent an awful lot of time trying to contact the mayors. Besides Paul's letters I sent out an email to all the mayors at the end of July."

"That's probably why you've had no response," retorted John, "I've heard your French and they probably couldn't understand a word of your email."

"I received one reply from the Director of External relations in Orleans, who sent an email to the local biking club with a copy to me to inform them about our ride. She also said they couldn't sponsor us. I also had a reply from the secretary of the mayor of Alencon giving the name and email address of the Twinning association president but stating that he was on holiday till August 15th. Unfortunately too late!" I stated.

"But we aren't going through Alencon so why did we get a reply from there?" Ray quizzed.

"We were initially but the route changed reducing our twinned towns by one. So one less mayor for you to worry about," replied Paul.

"I thought you sent out similar messages to all the Tourist Offices at the same time," said Ray.

"I did and had one reply from Gien saying I should get in touch with the mayor. I also sent an email to the mayors of all the British twinned towns."

"I hope that was in English," John laughed again, "or they would have been confused."

Didier drove on to an amazingly long aqueduct over La Loire and then to a mosaic museum where Didier talked non-stop to the Receptionist, whilst we walked round, so we would not have to pay. We finally drove back to Ouzouer with a road sign in the centre showing Great Ayton 980 kilometres away. "I think we've missed the mayor," Ray grinned. "At least John won't have to wear a GASBAGS shirt after all."

Didier and Jocelyne prepared another meal in the evening with ample wine. I can only say that again the French showed a very generous spirit and they made us feel very welcome.

Paul had planned that we would stop in a hotel in Argentan as our penultimate stopover before Calais. He had booked us in the Hotel de France, another Logis de France hotel, but had never had confirmation that our booking had been accepted for what was a Saturday night. So he was worried that we might arrive after a long day and find the hotel closed.

"Jocelyne, would you mind phoning up to check if we are booked in?" he asked.

After a rapid French exchange, Jocelyne announced that the hotel was shut on Saturday nights and that thus we weren't booked in. By this time I had adjourned to my bedroom, which was the dining room about one yard from where Jocelyne was on the phone. I had drunk more wine than I should have with Didier being very generous and keen that we try several vintages. I am always a perfect guest where wine is concerned and don't like to say no. I could vaguely see Paul and Didier checking the map. Paul stared at me to check I was still awake and asked, "Would you mind if we change the route and stay in Falaise instead?"

By this time my eyes were closed with doziness. Through my intoxicated state I could tell that Paul was slightly offended that I was taking no interest. I sat up pretending I was interested though my drink-confused brain was blaming Paul for not sorting this out before we left England (I am glad that thoughts cannot be read as Paul had put a great deal of effort into the arrangement of this ride). I heard Jocelyne on the phone again in a blur of French and she booked us a hotel in Falaise.

I lay back down again and slept peacefully. My biffon was rested and my thighs felt ready for the final push to the coast. We intended to leave at half past nine in the morning.

### Thurs September 2nd

Ouzouer-sur-Loire to Bonneval
74 miles Grand total 739 miles

The fanfares were out, the crowds lined the streets, the mayor gave us all a kiss on both cheeks, as we rode proudly out of Ouzouer in our GASBAGS shirts with heads held high—well I can dream! In fact Didier told us over breakfast that all the bikers that were to accompany us had found better things to do except for one, Daniel. "It does seem odd how our Ouzouer welcome has reduced at each occasion—almost like it is being manipulated," I said.

"Perhaps the mayor has intervened to ensure we don't get what looks like an official welcome," remarked Ray.

"I doubt it," said Paul, ever protective of the Twinning Associations. "This is a weekday and most people will have to work."

"The bloody mayor doesn't work—his role is to entertain. Where is he?" sniggered John.

"You two couldn't organise a piss-up in a brewery," Ray grinned, pointing at Paul and myself.

"I will cycle with you as far as St Benoit-sur-Loire to swell your cavalcade. I've not cycled for a long time so be gentle with me," Didier said smiling. "I will have to use Amelie's bike—it's a bit small as I bought it her when she was fourteen. My knees will be around my neck."

We loaded up our bikes and were almost ready to go when Daniel cycled up on his racing bike. He looked to be mid-fifties, was wearing the Ouzouer biking club shirt and shorts, and had thighs like tree trunks. "Bonjour," he called.

Paul went up to him, shook his hand, and began a long conversation in French. "What was that all about?" I asked Paul when they had finished.

"Daniel cycled from Biarritz to Perpignan earlier this year. The ride was across eleven peaks in the Pyrenees and he cycled a distance of seven hundred and twenty-five kilometres. I told him I would love to do that next year."

"Would your wife give you a pass-out for three weeks again next year?" I queried.

"She's marvellous—she'd even accompany me in the car. In fact my whole family could act as my backup."

"She sounds like an angel to me Paul. Are you sure?"

"Positive!"

After thanking Jocelyne for her remarkable hospitality, we set off with Paul, Ray and myself wearing GASBAGS shirts. Didier led us down the main street so we waved at all the passers-by but the only ones that waved back were two young children in pushchairs—perhaps they hadn't understood the mayor's directive that we weren't an official tour.

We arrived at St Benoit-sur-Loire and stopped outside the Basilica. Didier gathered us round him to explain its history, with Paul translating. "This is the only survival of a famous monastery founded in the seventh century to which the relics of St Benedict were brought from Monte Cassino. The Basilica was built started in the early eleventh century and completed in the early thirteenth century. In the crypt, a modern shrine contains the remains of St Benedict, which still attracts many pilgrims."

Didier turned back at this point and we set off again with Daniel leading. As we cycled out of St Benoir we passed massive fields growing beetroot. Daniel turned to me and said proudly, "St Benoir grows almost all the beetroot for the whole of France. It is a great source of fibre, contains no fats and has very few calories so is very popular."

I questioned Daniel, "I am surprised that beetroot is grown right next to the Ouzouer nuclear power station. Doesn't anyone complain?"

"No, it is quite normal to grow vegetables adjacent to nuclear power stations in France. We have the world's largest nuclear power generator on a per capita basis, and rank second in total installed nuclear capacity behind the United States."

"I thought you were much more reliant on nuclear power than the UK."

"Yes, currently, about 77% of France's electricity comes from the fifty-eight nuclear reactors."

"It's frightening—one Chernobyl in France could have an enormous impact on Britain."

"I work alongside Didier. You shouldn't worry. Our technology is quite safe."

"I see—that explains how you know all the facts about France's nuclear energy."

When we reached Chateauneuf-sur-Loire, Daniel turned back after shaking our hands.

The ride had been flat up to now and continued to be flat all the way to Bonneval. This part of France reminded me of East Anglia and I assumed must be classed as the food basket of France.

"Fantastic easy ride now," I remarked, "Very few cars and we can cycle alongside each other, have a chat, and get in the true GASBAGS spirit."

"Don't include me in GASBAGS," remarked John scowling.

"You don't do enough gasbagging so we wouldn't have you," I laughed. "The dictionary definition of a gasbag is someone who chatters too much."

"I'm glad I've not got verbal diarrhoea like most GASBAGS members," John smirked.

"I think it is much too flat here. My perfect cycle ride was the one we did in June 2002 around Mull. The mountain and sea views were wonderful, the lack of traffic was a joy, and the cycle ride was mainly undulating until we approached Tobermory, where we had to push our bikes up two hills that were each worse than an Alpine pass," said Paul.

"I enjoyed that one as well," I said. "It was great. I remember that we had continuous rain on the way there, then as soon as we caught the boat across the sun came out and we frazzled for four days. All fourteen who went really enjoyed it."

I felt like relieving myself and looked round for some cover but there was absolutely none as the landscape was flat for miles. So I just stood by the side of the road and pointed Percy at the pavement. I thought people passing would assume I was French as I had often passed Frenchmen peeing by the side of motorways on previous trips to France. I had almost finished, a fairly long effort after all my refreshment from the water bottles, when I heard a car approaching. I turned, with Percy still firmly gripped, to see four young attractive women smiling at me and pointing as if they had never seen one before. I smiled back nonchalantly.

The weather had started brightly but never went beyond being a pleasant temperature for cycling with spots of rain around four as we approached Bonneval. It turned out to be a very attractive little village with canals running along side some of the streets like a mini-Amsterdam and with medieval buildings. We easily found our hotel, The Hotel de France, as it was on the main street in between a bar and a shop. The hotel was very attractive, painted cream with open brown shutters on the three double windows above a conservatory, and was surrounded by flower tubs containing various bushes.

Paul jumped off his bike and strode up to the front door all ready to practice his French. He knocked and knocked then tried the door and it was locked. "No one here," he called, "I can't believe it. I've heard of a hotel having skeleton staff but not dead staff," he laughed loudly. "I will check in the restaurant next door."

He re-appeared after a time. "They don't open until five. We may as well look round."

So we strolled around and came back at five and tried again. This time the door was opened and we trooped into the almost dark restaurant and were given the keys to our rooms, which were on the floor above. I led the way into the dark staircase and pushed the light switch. I was almost at the room when the light went out and we were in complete darkness. "Bloody stupid this," I shouted, as we all groped around on the walls to find the upstairs switch.

"I can't understand why they have timers on their lights. It's very customer unfriendly," Paul said.

"The hotel seems to be empty—perhaps that is why," responded John.

"I've found the switch," shouted Ray.

"I can tell as the light has just come on," laughed John, as he rushed to the room.

"We are in," I said to Paul. "Did you check about eating?"

"This is another of the Logis de France hotels that appears to be prefer that you eat elsewhere even though they serve food."

"Perhaps they get a fixed wage not linked to how many people eat in."

"Yes—crazy situation. They recommended one quite a walk down the street—claimed the food was excellent."

I wrote my report and sent it off. "Jeff has sent us an email. He is arranging a big arrival for our return night."

"I want to attend but I must see my family that first night back. See if he will move it. I want to be there—I don't want to miss out on a big celebration."

"Don't worry it is likely that Jeff is vastly exaggerating and that there will only be a few GASBAGS."

We strolled down the road with most houses being decked with flowers. "What's the population of this place?" Ray asked, "It's very attractive with all the flowers and looks to be quite big."

"Surprisingly the population is only about the same as Great Ayton—around 4,500," I replied, "the town has an excellent website that gives the town's details."

We found the recommended restaurant. It had a good atmosphere though very few customers. When the food arrived it was like 'nouvelle cuisine' with one piece of carrot, and two small bits of potato on the plate besides the meat. As we had found at all restaurants, sliced baguettes were served for no charge. We decided against buying wine but each had a coffee, but were astounded when the bill came as the price of 'grande cafe au lait' was more than £3 each, and the carafe of house wine cost less.

As we sauntered back John remarked, "I have begun to feel quite safe in these twinned towns now—the possibility of meeting a mayor seems to be negligible. Just four to go."

"So you must have checked the website at least once to know this place is twinned," I responded. "It is actually twinned to Westerham, which is very close to the M25 going round London and on the Kent/Surrey border."

"That's must be only just over three hundred away so perhaps the twinning is active," Ray came in, happy to use his Ordnance Survey skills.

"I wouldn't have minded Great Ayton being twinned with this place," remarked Paul.

"I enjoyed being 'Mapman' today. I always feel that bit safer being 'Mapman' knowing I certainly can't get lost," I grinned.

"Those daily printouts you gave us of the route were excellent Paul, but there's no doubt that the Michelin guide is required as well by the route leader each day," John remarked.

"A good idea of yours Paul that the route leadership should rotate daily," I said. "Whose turn is it tomorrow?"

"Mine," replied Ray.

"Well don't forget to wait for the slowest," I said.

"That sounds like a self-interest statement—it is bound to be you," Ray laughed.

### Friday September 3rd

Bonneval to Belleme
47 miles Grand total 786 miles

I expected that this day was going to be an easy day as Paul estimated 41 miles. First Paul and I took some photographs of the canals, whilst Ray and John waited patiently—surprisingly I never heard them complain once. A scene on one canal bridge was idyllic—the bridge was decked with white and pink flowers, there were trees either side of the canal, and trees reflecting in the water. In fact all the bridges that we crossed were decked with flowers, not something you would find in England, though we do deck out our roundabouts well. Perhaps we care more for the car owner than the pedestrian.

The ride started well, not as flat as the previous day but with gently sloping ups and downs. We passed one very grand massive house with at least four turrets and very intricate brickwork, which I don't think was a chateau There is one like it in Great Ayton next to the cemetery but less than a tenth of the size and only one turret—some of our houses are not on the same scale.

We reached Nogent-le-Rotrou after 32 miles. I said, "About time we stopped for lunch as there's only nine miles to go."

"Ah," Paul responded, "I may have made a slight mistake on my calculation. We still have fifteen miles to go."

"That's not far with it being so flat," John remarked.

"How about eating in that transport café type of restaurant over there," Ray said.

The restaurant was very long inside and must have had twenty tables at least with most being full and all having at least one cheap-looking bottle of wine. There was a standard menu of a buffet starter of all sorts of cold salad type food, followed by steak and chips, followed by cheese, followed by a sweet, followed by coffee.

"What value," exclaimed John, our accountant, "All that for just ten Euros—that only seven pounds. Who said France was expensive!"

"Not only that," responded Paul, "We can drink as much wine as we like. Have you seen that most people are leaving half-full bottles of wine when they leave."

"It is like it is being treated like water," Ray said.

"Well it's not water and we still have fifteen miles to go in this heat so I'm not indulging," I declared.

The rest agreed. I left a tip with the manageress looking astounded, as I doubt she would get many tips. As we came out of the restaurant the sun came out with the temperature being over 28 DegC, so we decided to collapse in the grounds of a church for an hour just up the road.

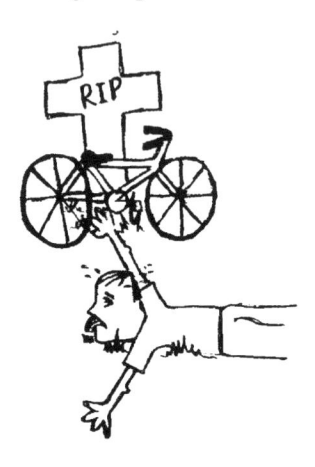

I took a short walk up to a new swimming pool that had just been built. I hoped to get a swim, but I was informed in French, which I just understood, that it had not yet been opened. When I arrived back Paul and John were stretched out topless absorbing the sun whilst Ray had retreated to the shade provided by the church wall.

"The pool is not yet open. It looks to be rather grand for this small village," I remarked.

"It's not that small," said Paul. "I believe its population is over 7,000. It has quite a history. It was formerly the capital of the district of Perche. It has a castle over one thousand years old. I looked round it a few years ago."

We set off again and suddenly the ups and downs became much steeper, like we were back on the Pyrenean fingers. Ray and John looked much happier, and suddenly Paul was off like a madman surging up the hills. I trudged up rather slowly praying that the next hill would be the last but saw the next one in front as soon as I reached the top of one. There was even one instance when I could see the road stretching out for miles in front with two long hills in view. Paul, John and Ray stopped on one intersection to let me catch up. I stopped and wrung out my sweatband and drank half a pint of water.

Paul remarked, "What wonderful scenery."

"It looks little different to yesterday except the immense sweetcorn-filled fields are sloping," I replied feeling exhausted.

We finally arrived at Belleme and what I thought would be an easy day had turned difficult with the extra six miles and the hot weather. As we arrived a large truck carrying a real camel and a llama held us up and it seems that we had reached Belleme just in time for the festival that was to start the following day. But we were moving on! Belleme had a medieval character and was quite pretty with narrow streets and old houses with coloured shutters, but when we searched for a 'pub' we found only three of which only one opened onto the street.

The Hotel that we were booked in was another Logis de France hotel, Hotel Le Relais St Louis. After the experience of previous Logis de France hotels my expectations were not very high—lights had been on timers going out at inappropriate times, the staff encouraging us to eat elsewhere and some locked up when we arrived. But this hotel certainly looked magnificent. It was painted in pinky-orange with white surrounds for the windows, had three floors with each floor having seven full height brown Georgian windows, and had flower baskets hung from each window. Paul had booked us in for half board so we did not need to search out where to eat. Inside the service we received was excellent—but the room lighting was so poor that I had to sit on the toilet seat again to type the daily report. By the time I came off the throne the other three were seated downstairs in the dining room drinking beer and getting impatient to order the food.

The meal was excellent and waitresses were very attentive. We all felt very relaxed and for once drank wine. "A fantastic view as we came into Belleme," I remarked. "What was the forest?"

"That is the renowned oak forest of Belleme," Paul replied. "This place is much smaller than you would think. When I booked the hotel I found that the population was only about 2,000—surprising when it has such an excellent hotel."

"I believe it is twinned with Goring in South Oxfordshire. I had read on the Goring website that there is an active programme of exchange visits," I said.

"Must be only four hundred miles," remarked our Ordnance Survey expert Ray.

"I've just received an email from an old friend of mine in Australia who I had told about our ride. She's been reading the diary on a daily basis. She said what an extraordinary achievement and that she didn't realize I had it in me," I said.

"You almost don't," chuckled Ray, "what with your new nickname of L'escargot—the snail!"

"She said I might have started something with all the inspirational commentary."

"What inspirational comment? What have you been saying? It can't have been about us," Paul laughed.

"She says she joined a couple of girlfriends in a ride today and that it nearly killed her. It made her realize how unfit she was and that she needs padded bike pants to survive another bike ride. She was surprised that we weren't wearing padded shorts."

"I don't wear padded shorts. I like to feel the saddle," remarked Paul.

"Ray and mine are padded," said John, "but they look on the outside like standard training shorts—quite expensive."

"I know," I said, "I bought some. Unfortunately the first time I wore them I splashed water on them when cleaning my teeth. It looked like I'd peed down them. I couldn't imagine how bad they would look with my sweat."

"I can imagine," laughed Ray. "Like you had forgotten to take your shorts down when going to the toilet."

"Well I've stuck to my three pairs of standard padded black biking shorts, rotating them each day. I even have a pair of padded underpants, which I have worn on alternate days. They certainly make a difference. You must have no feeling in your bum Paul," I said.

"I just raise my bum off the saddle whenever it feels a bit sore," Paul responded.

"I do that as well. My gell saddle has been very comfortable with the hole in the centre—maintains my fertility," I said.

"I thought you were like me—being in the IOFB club—I only fire blanks," Ray remarked. "I use one of the hard leather seats that moulds to your backside—very comfortable."

"It takes endless miles for them to mould. I'm sure you came out of your mother's womb with a biker's bum," John laughed.

"Well my Australian friend sends her congratulations to us all," I said. "We can now claim we have a growing international audience what with Naoko in Japan and your friends in Australia, Paul. This ride is certainly helping you achieve your target of 10,000 miles this year,."

"I am hoping I can cycle that far—I certainly want to beat the 9,300 miles that I cycled in a year at the age of nineteen," Paul replied.

"You certainly put some effort into it with those long rides of 125 miles then 152 miles in a day. I was getting worried. Either you would be too fit or drop down dead with exhaustion. In either case the trip might have become a one-man cycle ride! This was before you two got involved," I said looking at Ray and John.

"I wouldn't have completed the 154 miles if you hadn't come out to help me with the last few miles," Paul replied. "I became worried after finishing those rides as I had what I nicknamed 'White Penis syndrome'—my penis had shrunk to a tiny white blob. I named it after 'Vibration White finger', which is a form of Raynaud's Disease."

"I know about Raynard's Disease. It is caused by a restriction in the blood supply to the extremities, usually the fingers and toes. The parts initially turn white and dead looking and then become inflamed. An attack may be accompanied by significant pain, numbness or a tingling sensation. It normally affects women," Ray said.

"Well I am all man," grinned Paul. "Though when I looked at my penis after the rides I thought I might be changing sex. Vibration White Finger is caused by working with vibrating machinery such as grinders and drills where the fingers may go into spasm. This is due to an intermittent lack of blood supply to the fingers. I thought my title was very suitable."

"It is not surprising that cyclists have fertility problems. You lot have all been chopped off so it won't affect you. And I don't care—I don't want any children," John stated.

# Normandy

Normandy gets its name from the Viking Norsemen who sailed up the river Seine in the 9th century. The quintessential image of Normandy is of a lush, pastoral region of apple orchards and contented cows, cider and pungent cheeses—but the region also spans the windswept beaches of the Cotentin and the wooded banks of the Seine valley.

Memories of the D-Day Landings of 1944, still linger along the Cote de Nacre and the Cotentin Peninsula. 45,000 Allied troops poured ashore on to these magnificent beaches in the closing weeks of World War II. The Battle of Normandy followed and after several months and 100,000 deaths, German resistance was finally broken.

Normandy is blessed with a mild maritime climate, with few temperature extremes. Summer begins in mid-June with temperatures in the mid to upper twenties. These temperatures sometimes last through September and into early October.

I had been to the Caen port many times on the way back to England but I had never actually looked round the Caen town centre, so had never seen the great 11th-century abbey churches built by William the Conqueror and his queen, Matilda. Perhaps this time! However I had walked round a few war cemeteries and seen the Bayeux tapestry, the story of William's invasion of England. I do have a photograph of my wife (of twenty-four years but now ex I'm sad to say) and two sons in front of the island of Mont-St-Michel just before we walked round all the narrow alleyways.

### Saturday September 4th

Belleme to Falaise
67 miles Grand total 853 miles

I had washed my clothes the night before even though there was a large sign, 'No clothes to be washed in the bedrooms'. I felt sure that this sign could not apply to cyclists as the all the French love cyclists. The sign should probably have said, "'No clothes to be washed in the bedrooms—this does not apply to cyclists'. However, in the morning the clothes were still very damp, especially the shorts, so I put them all in a plastic bag.

I carried all my bags downstairs and pushed my bike out of the hotel and leaned it against the hotel wall. I thought I must wring out my clothes. I had just started on my shorts when the hotel manager appeared—a middle-aged attractive woman. Paul immediately began to talk to her—though she looked too old compared to his earlier fancies. He had her name off her in a jiffy, 'Francoise'. I continued to wring out my clothes though she was standing only a metre away and water was splashing on her shoes. I thought it was better to act innocent, and to not appear guilty by rapidly shoving away my wet clothes. Her English was very good so I remarked, "What a wonderful hotel. Last night's meal was excellent." It was only then that I noticed out of the corner of my eye that Paul had stepped back a few paces, and was grinning. I packed my clothes and we all set off, waving to the hotel manager.

John burst into fits of laughter. "That was fantastic. You were so nonchalant."

Paul followed John in laughing. "The poor woman didn't know what to say. Her feet must have been wet through by the time you had finished."

"She probably fancied you, Mike," Ray said. "She looked the sort that would like tall receding slightly-podgy Englishmen."

For me this was the best day of cycling and was alike to cycling around Great Ayton and Stokesley. The route was mainly flat with minor slopes for the first 20 miles before any serious hills arrived. The road wound round small villages, and the views on either side were interesting with lush grass covered hills and forests. The temperature was 30 DegC and I drank over three litres of water on the way.

Around one o'clock we reached Exres. "How about stopping for lunch in that bar," remarked Ray. "I am starving."

"I will check if they serve," our French expert Paul said, and jumped off his bike and disappeared into the bar.

"If he appears with another bloody ice-cream I will go crazy," I remarked.

After a few minutes Paul reappeared. "Yes they serve food. The choice is pate and lasagne for 10 Euros, about £7, or nothing."

"I am not keen on nothing," Ray replied. "I'm on for the pate and lasagne."

"Be careful when you step inside the door. Every time you step on the mat it goes beep," and Paul stepped backwards with a loud beep emanating through the door.

So each of us strode into the bar and a loud beep emanated out. "It was not possible to not step on the mat," remarked Ray plaintively at the surly landlady though it was obvious she didn't understand a word.

We sat down at a table just inside the door and ordered large beers with the food. There were four other customers standing around the bar drinking and smoking of which one was an attractive slim woman aged about thirty with blond curly hair. "I detest smokers in pubs," I whispered to Paul in a loud enough whisper to be overheard. However I assumed I would have no reaction since I didn't expect locals in such a remote part of France would speak English.

"I agree," he replied. "The dreadful smell gets entangled in your clothes and then you need to wash them so you don't smell like an ashtray."

"I've kissed some women who smoked," I replied. "It is almost like licking an ashtray. Yuck! I think pubs should pay to have your clothes washed—that would soon make them become non-smoking."

Paul was closest to the four customers. He turned round and struck up a conversation in French with one of the men. The other French joined in and I realised that the woman could speak English and with Paul concentrating on the men for once I asked the woman, "What do you do?"

"Not much right now. I was a child minder but got fed up with the job—too much hassle. I met Michel who lives on a farm near here and moved in with him," she replied.

"Are you enjoying your life better now?" I asked.

"Not really. It is all very slow around here. I would like more excitement. I hope to visit England. Would you like to exchange some emails?"

I was surprised about this request as I couldn't imagine there being many PC's around this part of France but I gave her my email address. I felt sure that Naoko would not be jealous since this woman was much too young for me.

Our food arrived and we turned back to face John and Ray. "What was the man saying," John asked. "He looked to be concerned on our behalf."

"He warned us to watch out for the gendarmerie as they are aware that we entered this bar after parking our bikes. It seems that that there are so few crimes around here that the slightest sway back and forth on our bikes and we could be prosecuted for undue care and attention."

We stopped at a War memorial on the way into Falaise, and read that in July and August 1944 there were major battles around Falaise when France was liberated. "One of my dad's friends who is in the British Legion but was too young to have fought in the Second World War, used to go on coach tours around all the Allied cemeteries—a strange holiday pastime. He even brought back a plate, which he gave as a gift to my parents, that showed the D-Day beaches and referenced Falaise," I stated.

"My wife's uncle fought in the war around these parts and he mentioned Falaise in particular. He often told us detailed stories about the battles. It really sparked my interest so I read more about it," said Paul. "Have you heard of the Falaise pocket?"

"Is it a special suit pocket?" asked Ray vaguely.

"No! It was part of the battle for Normandy, the definitive battle of the Western Front in July and August 1944. Throughout the intense struggle for control of the Falaise Pocket, the Allied air forces were wreaking horrendous destruction on the Germans inside. While thousands of Germans were able to slip out of the trap, almost no tanks or vehicles survived. The Allies managed to capture almost one half of the Wehrmacht and its equipment then in Normandy."

"It's hard to believe how many hundreds and thousands died around here when it now looks so peaceful," I said sadly.

Paul responded, "I stopped for a short time about a mile back. I closed my eyes and tried to imagine the destruction and horror that there must have been around here. From what I read the main allied troops involved in these battles were Canadian though British, Polish, Dutch, Belgian, and Czech formations were also involved. The fighting was savagely intense."

"I've tried that same technique of closing my eyes. I went to Knossos in Crete where the Minoan civilisation existed over 3,500 years ago. I tried to imagine how life must have been—very difficult. I always liked to search out for the toilets," I said.

"What for? I thought you would use fields like you have on this ride," Ray chortled.

"Not those sort of toilets. The ancient toilets! I like to understand have ancient civilisations got rid of their faeces."

We arrived at the hotel which was a three storey light pink painted building with white window shutters all open, giving a feeling of freshness. I immediately wrote my daily report and the other three disappeared across the road to a park. I found them later stretched out watching an outdoor wedding. "Just look at the men," whispered Paul. "They all have thick-set necks and broad shoulders—I think they could be Mafia."

"He almost waded into to stop the wedding," John laughed. "He wanted to save the petite bride from those brutish-looking men."

"What stopped you then?" I enquired.

"I realised I was keen to live," grinned Paul.

We strolled back to the hotel and decided to eat in the hotel. We had our most expensive meal to celebrate our last night sleeping in France. As we were eating we heard a noise outside. We all turned to stare out of the window. "Look at all those cars—they're making quite a din," Ray remarked.

"It's the procession for the wedding," Paul responded. "I've seen this kind of procession elsewhere in France."

"I'm surprised. I thought the French were more restrained. I can imagine this kind of noise in Latin countries like Italy and Spain," John said.

"Did you see that there is a circus performing in Falaise?" Paul remarked.

"I'm not going to a circus—I'm too old," Ray replied.

"They seem to be quite common in France—I've seen them advertised in other towns," I said.

"Yes, you are right. There are many more circuses in France than in the UK. I read an article recently saying that there are twenty-one in France as compared with just nine in the UK," Paul responded.

I laughed. "Perhaps that's because us English have a love of animals whilst the French love eating anything that moves including horses, frogs and snails."

"What's that to do with a circus," murmured John.

"Not a lot—I was just making an observation. Don't be so bloody petty."

After the meal we strolled around Falaise, passing a statue of William the Conqueror. "It seems William the Conqueror was born in Falaise in 1028," John said reading the plaque next to the statue.

"All I know about him is that he conquered England in 1066 to become William I," I said.

"I expect that Falaise uses William as a tourist icon in the same way as Great Ayton uses Captain Cook," Paul said.

"There's a funny story about Captain Cook. His parent's house in Great Ayton was sold to Australia and shipped stone by stone many years ago. They never told the Aussies that their discoverer never ever slept in the house," I said laughing.

We strolled into the main square with several outdoor restaurants, and realised that we could have eaten more substantial food for half the price. We bought a round of large beers and began to soak up the French atmosphere from the packed tables around us. "So how might this great achievement affect you all?" I asked.

Paul replied," I intend to follow Daniel in riding across the Pyrenees."

"I've given it no thought," said John.

"I would like to cycle off-road round Iceland," replied Ray.

"You should read Josie Dew's book about cycling around Iceland. It might put you off," I said. "It is really tough."

"How's this achievement going to affect you then Mike?" Paul asked.

"I've really enjoyed this trip but I would prefer routes that are not as challenging as we encountered in the south of France."

I had written my daily report earlier and when we arrived back in the hotel I tried to send it off. The phones in the room worked but kept disconnecting from the Internet. I asked downstairs at the reception if I could attach to their phone-line. In broken English (the receptionist's not mine) I understood that her phone-line had no wall connector. I realised that it would not be possible to send a report, the first day that this had happened. My worldwide audience (two in Australia, one in Japan, one in Switzerland, and several in Middlesbrough) would not get another report until the ship docked in England.

## Sunday September 5th

Falaise to Caen
61 miles Grand total 914 miles

I woke up thinking that this would be a wonderfully short day with Falaise being just 25 miles from Caen, and add on the 10 miles to the ferry terminal at Ouistreham would make a nice short flat ride.

"Hey they've got Kelloggs Cornflakes. My favourite," I said as we sat down for breakfast.

"They taste like cardboard," replied John. "I'm on for porridge."

"I used to be called the 'Cornflake kid' when I was young as I had a big bowl for breakfast and one when I arrived home from school," I said.

"Perhaps that's why you turned into a two metre lamppost," John smiled.

"You should have had some then. Your legs are so short they are dangling in the air sitting on that chair," I replied, not to be outdone.

"It is going to be hot today—up to 31 DegC," Ray announced.

"That's great. Perhaps we can relax on the beach—we've only got a short day," I said.

"Not that short," Paul responded. "I thought we should enjoy this day by going on a really scenic route through Suisse-Normandy. It's going to be less than sixty miles."

"Are you sure you aren't just taking us on a long route to add more miles towards your 10,000 mile goal. It's going to be tough in this heat," I complained.

"You'll just have to wring out your sweatband more often," Ray laughed. "I'm glad I don't sweat like you. I still have water in one of my water bottles that's been there since Biarritz. You must be more French than English with the amount of French water you've drunk, Mike."

"Sweating keeps your skin looking young and healthy doesn't it Paul," I said, looking for support from my equally sweaty room-partner.

"I absolutely agree. It's not stopped hair loss unfortunately," responded Paul. "How have you kept all your hair John?"

"He's never had to baby-make," laughed Ray. "It comes out on the front if the man's on top and on the back if the woman's on top."

"You must've done both then," I laughed loudly. "You've had enough partners."

"We're going through three twinned towns today," Paul said changing the subject. "You'll be in and out of a GASBAGS shirt all day long when the mayors greet us John."

"The odds are rather against us meeting any so I am not worried. We've passed thirteen twinned towns without even a sniff of a mayor," John replied.

We stopped for a short break at Pont d'Ouilly, a little town full of flowers and greenery at the confluence of the rivers Orne and Noireau, which had a lovely feeling of peace and serenity. We stood on the bridge and looked down on the canoes going up and down. "I never realised that there were such picturesque little villages so close to Caen," I remarked. "I have always driven past on the way to the Vendee or the Dordogne."

"This parts lovely. You can see why it's called Suisse-Normandy. I have brought my family to this area a few times," Paul responded.

"I thought you had to go all the way to the Dordogne to get good canoeing but now I know better," I said.

I began pedalling slowly across the bridge and realised that my chain had come off and was wedged tight against the wheel. Ray came across and held my bike whilst I pulled like mad and finally released the chain. My hands were black with oil but fortunately I had a packet of 'Wet-ones' (Paul's idea to bring) and they worked wonders.

After gazing for quite a time at this pleasant scene we were about to cycle on, and I inserted one of my biking shoes in the peddle cleat then put my other shoe on the pedal and it caught in the other cleat. I lost my balance and fell outwards onto the road in the path of oncoming cars. A Frenchman bravely jumped out in front of the cars, and stopped them whilst I slowly extricated myself from underneath the bike. I jumped up shouting, "Merci, merci" whilst the other team members, whilst initially concerned now found my fall highly amusing.

We cycled on past more massive fields of sweetcorn, and I began talking to my camcorder as I cycled and filmed, "I love sweetcorn. I love France. I love sweetcorn..." Was I getting demob happy? We stopped for lunch on a very scenic road running next to the River Orne on the bottom road through Clecy. Flowers lined the side of the road and canoes were going up and down and there were several restaurants. I was passed by one of the trucks that go up and down to collect groups of canoes, so there must be a pre-determined pick-up point.

"About time we stopped to eat," Ray announced always keen to eat regularly.

"We seem to be eating non-stop," I said.

"We're expending vast amounts of calories cycling. It's important that we have big lunches and dinners," Ray replied.

"If we continue at home like we have been doing we'll all turn into balloons," John chortled.

"That restaurant looks good—it's right next to the river. There are some enormous ice-creams being served," Paul said patting his stomach. "I didn't come here to lose weight."

So we sat down under massive umbrellas and watched the canoes go by slowly on the river. For once Paul and I had a large beer each. The service was the slowest yet and we must have been there almost two hours. We all finished with the enormous mouth-watering ice creams.

"Is this road all there is to Clecy?" asked Ray.

"No, the main village is up the hill though it's only got a population of just over a thousand," Paul replied. "That's why we've not met the mayor. He's probably waiting for us up there now."

"I won't need to get changed then. I was looking forward to wearing a GASBAGS shirt," John smiled.

"Still plenty of opportunity. This place is twinned to Ermington near Plymouth—the Clecy website says there is a joint kayak club," I said.

"Not too surprising," Ordnance Survey Ray responded. "They are very close—just 200 miles by road and a ferry from Poole to Cherbourg."

At Clecy we had ridden 18 miles and I thought it was a mere 25 miles more to Caen, which didn't seem too bad. We cycled along fast with the wind behind us and made good progress. Then Paul, who was 'Mapman' for the day, stopped and we all drew up next to him. "What's wrong," I asked.

"I've missed a turn. We need to go back two miles," Paul replied.

"I'm not going back," I said in an ill-tempered voice. "That looks to be a fast road in front."

"Well you can go that way Mike," Ray intervened, "but I'm following Paul. That's the motorway that leads straight into Caen. Have you seen the speed of the cars?"

I looked and now realised I was being stupid. "Sorry Paul. I guess even you can make mistakes. It is surprising what sun, sweat and hills can do to one's temperament."

So we all turned round and that added an extra four miles. As we cycled past the Thury Harcourt village sign I shouted, "John—get changed fast. This could be our first mayor."

Paul shouted, "Look there's a crowd waiting for us."

"Who are you kidding," replied John. "That's the queue for the toilet. Surprising they've got a public toilet as it only looks to be a small place."

"They're probably admiring the dumps around the hole," said Ray earthily.

"It is only a small village—it has a population of about two thousand," Paul said.

"It's twinned with Seaton in Devon—I found a reference to it on the Thury website," I said.

"That's even closer than the Clecy twinned town of Ermington," Ray said. "It's odd that the further south you go in France then the further north the twinned town is in the UK."

"I hadn't realised that," Paul responded. "It must lead to more active twinning in the south of England compared to the north—a shame—the old north-south divide."

"Did this village suffer much damage in the last war?" John asked.

"It was almost destroyed," Paul replied. "My wife's uncle was also involved in the fighting around here. In mid-August 1944 it was still occupied by the Germans. The British were told that they had to enlarge the bridgehead over the River Orne and had to take Thury-Harcourt as soon as possible to allow for the Falaise pocket to be closed."

"I remember that now," said Ray smiling.

Paul continued, "On the day they attacked they suffered many casualties and the Germans counter-attacked. Finally the British had to withdraw leaving Thury-Harcourt in flames. The following day the British came back again to find the village empty and moved in among the ruins of still burning buildings—it seems that the Germans had suffered very high casualties and withdrawn at the same time as the British. The German's withdrawal had been complete, and was marked by unnecessary acts of destruction. The beautiful 17th century chateau was a smoking ruin."

"Was it ever rebuilt?" I asked.

"Unfortunately all that remains is the main frontage and a few other parts. That must be it over there," Paul said and pointed.

Just before Caen we passed the 900-mile mark and stopped at a roundabout sign with one exit saying Caen. We propped all four bikes up against the road sign all pointed in the same direction—forward to show off the identical bags. "Let's take some photographs to prove we made it," Paul said.

"I'll take them," John said.

"A shame we can't get you on them John," I said, "We've worked well as a team."

Paul stood next to the signpost hands-in pocket and bare topped. Ray was in a dark green top with his hat on and his 'Ray Le Pong' dog tag dangling round his neck. I had on my GASBAGS shirt. We were all, of course, in shorts. I had pulled mine up a bit in hopes I could get more of my legs brown.

"What about us all wearing GASBAGS shirts? That's the same shirt and shorts you wore in Biarritz isn't it Ray—have you ever washed them?" I asked.

"A few times. I'm not rummaging in my bags for my GASBAGS shirt—I'm too tired," Ray said. "That's looks like the same GASBAGS shirt that you were wearing in Biarritz."

"I have two," I replied. "With my sweat I've been washing them each day and rotating."

"I want to show my brown torso—who knows Julie or Muriel might see these photographs," Paul smiled.

"If they did they might be sick," I laughed.

"For heaven sake don't put on your hat Mike," Ray said. "It stinks—you are supposed to wash them you know. I'm washed mine several times."

"I didn't know you were supposed to wash hats," I laughed. "I thought there'd been a funny smell around my face for a few days. It was only when I sniffed it after it fell off at that last roundabout that I realised how smelly it was."

"I suggest you don't wear it again until you get home—any woman wanting to embrace you as we re-enter England would be put off," Paul said laughing loudly.

"I remember one holiday a few years ago in France when my son wore the same trainers every day for three weeks. On the way home he took them off and we almost suffocated. We made him hang them out of the car window—fortunately the smell is not as bad as that," I said.

"Let's get on with these photographs. You're like a group of women talking," John the photographer pleaded.

"You should take one of the four bikes lined up with the bags showing. Perhaps we can get Altura to sponsor us," Paul stated—not keen to miss a trick.

We cycled onto towards Caen and decided to go into the Caen itself to find a bar where we could celebrate the end of the ride. I had been on the Caen ferry many times in the past but had never driven into the Caen centre. "Caen is much bigger than I had thought," I said. "It would be easy to get lost."

"It's not much smaller than Middlesbrough with its population being over 100,000," Paul replied.

"How did you know that," I asked.

"I found out when I checked the Caen website. Let's take the signs for the City Centre," Paul said.

"All the bars are closed," John stated.

"It is a Sunday," Ray responded.

"There's bound to be some open near the Abbeys. This way," Paul shouted.

We reached the two famous Abbeys and close by we found several pavement bars crowded with people. Paul asked for a pint of beer (we had learnt to say "grande" beer otherwise you were given less than half a pint) and for a large orange juice. I asked for the same and then asked for the same again later with my bill coming to over £10, and having been spent in less than quarter of an hour.

"That's bloody expensive," I exclaimed.

"You should drink water to quench your thirst," Ray responded.

"You're right. It's just that spending euros never seems to be the same as spending pounds. About time we converted."

As I drank the beer I looked round and admired the two abbeys that could be easily seen from the bar. I turned to our French history expert. "Paul, you're bound to know the history of these abbeys."

"Yes I do. I've been to Caen several times with my family and looked round. Both of them were completed in the time of William the Conqueror, as was the Castle—we cycled past it. It's one of the largest medieval fortresses of Western Europe."

"So what's the difference between the Abbeys?" I asked.

"The Abbaye aux Hommes—for you Ray the Men's Abbey is the current town hall of Caen. It's dedicated to St Etienne. For a time in the late eighteenth century Napoleon turned it into a secondary school. The Abbaye aux Dames—for you Ray the Women's Abbey—is the current regional council of Basse-Normandie. It's dedicated to St Gilles."

"A right fount of knowledge, aren't you Paul," Ray stated looking slightly put out. "I know a few French words like 'Hommes' and 'Dames' you know. I'm not totally ignorant."

"A last chance to meet a mayor you two," John said looking at Paul and myself. "The Town Hall is just over there as you have just said Paul. I don't see any mayor rushing towards us. There are lots of little crowds about but they all appear to be ignoring us." John laughed.

"The mayor is allowed a day off you know. It is Sunday," Paul said and smiled sweetly. I could tell that nothing was going to interfere with his happiness of knowing he had made it.

"I bet this place is twinned with Portsmouth based on my observation that the more south you go in England the more north you can expect the twinned town to be in France," Ray observed.

"Spot on," I said. "Though funnily when I asked a website to check how far it was between the cities it came up with over 350 miles—the program had not been told about ferries! I hoped to see words like 'Jump in a boat and don't waste so much petrol'." I laughed.

"There's even a 'Caen Foundation' set up by Portsmouth whose objective is to enable young people under the age of twenty in Portsmouth to visit Caen for the purpose of developing social, cultural and recreational links with young persons there. I was impressed. I am involved with young people in my work role," Paul said.

"I was surprised to see that Caen is twinned with four other towns—Wurzburg in Germany, Nashville and Alexandria in the USA, and Thies in Senegal. Remarkable! It must take some organisation," I said.

"Don't be too surprised, Mike, as Middlesbrough is twinned with four towns—Dunkerque in France, Masvingo in Zimbabwe, Middlesboro in the USA, and Oberhausen in Germany," Paul responded.

We had to cycle the last 10 miles to the car ferry at Ouistreham. "It looks like we have to cycle down the motorway-like road," Paul said in his 'Mapman' role.

"I've driven on that road. It's not safe. Is there no other way?" I asked.

"No as far as I can tell," responded Paul.

So we set off tucking well into the right. After two miles I heard a car swerve and its horn was hit several times. "I was almost exterminated then," Ray shouted.

Going past the junctions was especially dangerous since the cars did not slow down at all when they went off. I passed one and a car shot on my inside with the driver shouting some obscenities at me with its horn blaring. I shouted to John who was just in front, "The French hospitality does not travel as far as their cars."

Once we reached the end of the motorway near the ferry terminal we discovered that there was a cycle path that runs parallel with the fast road. "I was almost killed back there! You're sacked 'Mapman'," Ray said to Paul jokingly.

We arrived at the Ferry terminal at five thirty and had six hours to wait for the departure of the Brittany Ferries ship. We found a restaurant where we consumed more beer and food and Paul locked up his bike to mine. When we emerged Paul could not find his key and searched his panniers. I began to imagine lifting our bikes as a pair, panniers attached, all the way onto the boat!

I sat in the Ferry terminal writing my report whilst Paul animatedly looked round the terminal area and had a drink at the bar, with the others sitting around looking bored. I asked each of them what they were looking forward to, and then wrote, "I am very happy that the day is over, and am ready for a good sleep on the boat. No more cycling for now—hurrah! hurrah! My biffon can stop taking any more punishment. Everyone feels a quiet sense of accomplishment, and now the hard work begins—collecting the sponsorship. Paul is looking forward to being back with his wife and sons. I am looking forward to talking again by phone to my partner in Japan, Naoko, and seeing my sons. Ray is looking forward to washing his clothes (not really Ray Le Pong!), and both Ray and John are looking forward to a good pint of English beer."

Our ferry was called and we cycled up to the terminal gate, expecting another wait. Paul spied some people in biking clothes in a car and strolled across for a chat. I went across after a time, as the wait was extensive. I thought I would find Paul boasting about how we had cycled across France. Instead he was in awe at the people in the car. It turned out that the two young men in the backseat were ranked fifth and seventh in the British cycling team. The father of one of them, who was the driver, had been in the 1964 British Olympic team in 1964. He explained that the team were lying third when he had touched another cyclist with his front wheel, with the slight delay moving the team into fourth.

Finally the gate opened and we cycled on-board and found our four-man bedroom. "Very small, John said. "At £95 each I had hoped they might have been bigger."

"Thanks for booking it John. Hope no-one snores," Ray said, "I need some sleep."

"Please yes please keep Mr Le Pong inactive Ray," I said jokingly.

"No striking a match in the morning," Paul laughed.

On this note John dived in the shower and the rest of us went for a noisy drink in the bar.

## Monday September 6th

Portsmouth to Great Ayton
300 miles by car

I awoke early and sneaked out with my laptop to make one last attempt to send my outstanding daily reports. I felt the story must get through. I first had breakfast and then opened my laptop and inserted the Blue-tooth card to link through my phone. I dialled out and after a time made a connection. I had almost sent the report when Ray rushed up to say we had to clear the cabin. I gave up. The worldwide audience would have to wait to read about the final two days. Would they think one of us had been injured or that a bike had collapsed? Would they get in touch with the French police just in case? Probably not!

The ferry docked and we went searching for the Hertz car hire offices and after asking several people found them after a good one-mile cycle. Ray and John signed for their estate car first, packed their bikes in the back and set off. Paul and I then obtained our car and requested insurance for both of us to drive although it was strictly my turn as Paul had driven down to Stansted Airport. I was not confident of staying awake for all the way back after a disturbed night's sleep. As we set off I remarked, "That's been much easier and cheaper than going back by train."

"It took some effort to decide on booking the cars though," Paul responded. "We ruled out our cars as we wouldn't be returning to the same location and the high airport car parking charges. Ray checked on taking a large van but ruled it out a non-starter as the cost was astronomic for a one-way trip as car hire companies only maintained a small fleet of these type of vans and so leaving them in a different location was charged at twice the price."

"When I checked on trains I read that it is now very difficult to get bikes on trains at all."

"We didn't have much of an option on the way down as the bikes had to be packed in those enormous boxes. There was no way we could have carried those from a station."

I drove initially whilst Paul was phoning all his business contacts about childcare problems. The car became a moving office. We arrived at Paul's house to collect his car then drove to Teesside Airport to drop off the hire car. As we arrived at my house Paul exclaimed, "What's that big notice on your gate?"

"A welcome home banner," I said. "There's only one person who would do that—Jeff!"

## "Le Tour de France

## Bonjour

## Welcome Home

## From GASBAGS"

"Well, after hoping that we might have had a welcome with banners in all the twinned towns, we finally have one at home," Paul laughed.

"Are you sure you can't call in tonight for our welcome home party?"

"I would love to but I need to spend time with my family. And the dog would be devastated."

The welcome home party that evening turned out to be from the Groupies (Jeff & Pam, Ray & Bridget) plus one other GASBAG. Just Ray and I turned up as Paul did stay with his family and John disappeared into his non-GASBAGS world.

"Thanks for the banner Jeff. I thought you said in your email that a big arrival party had been arranged. I was expecting the radio interviewers, journalists, photographers and half of Great Ayton and Stokesley," I laughed. "Where are they all?"

"I never really meant it," Jeff replied.

"You upset Paul that day. He thought he would miss out on being famous."

# Post-ride Activities

### Welcome Home

The following Thursday the full GASBAGS group met and we had our official welcome home and all of the team turned up, even John. However this was the last time Paul and I saw John for many weeks, which is a shame because the team spirit had been good on the ride with no real arguments. During the ride there had been little mention of the sponsorship raised though I did have a few digs at John for his lack of effort. I had little response though.

"I had a vision whilst we were doing this ride of where our epic journey might lead," I remarked in a loud voice trying to get attention amongst the beer-induced hubbub.

"What was this vision," asked John being less beer affected than the rest.

"Well it was based on the Calendar Girls film of the mature women who posed naked for a calendar. We could bring out a Calendar with all GASBAGS members being naked," I said.

"We would have to maintain our modesty—we could use bike pumps," Zoe laughed.

"Some women would have to use pint glasses to hide their boobies, though sherry glasses might do for some," Jeff gurgled and leered. "I want to take the photographs. Each month could be of a nude mixed couple."

"I had hoped that with all the effort we put into contacting the mayors that we would have met some and there would have been a few crowds cheering us along the way. I thought that the website would start to get lots of hits but it didn't," I said.

"Well we didn't meet any mayors and the biggest crowd was the queue for the toilet," John laughed.

"Mike had visions like this—he thrives on delusions," Ray said despairingly.

"I was very disappointed that we never met the Ouzouer mayor. I've met him. I thought he would have been courteous enough to meet a group of cyclists from his twinned town," Paul remarked.

"But just suppose that in Pau, our first twinned town, we had met the mayor and he had arranged a civic reception. He would have contacted the mayor of Agen, the next twinned town, who would have again arranged a civic reception. Our receptions would have snowballed," I said.

"That's a thought," Paul responded. "We should have spent more effort contacting the mayors at the start of the ride."

"I can see what might have happened," said Zoe, always one with ideas. "Mike would have transmitted back to the website the write-ups and photographs of the civic receptions. This would have prompted the towns' bike clubs to accompany you over the last few miles and to lead you through the cheering crowds. I've begun to get into this fantasy now." She laughed.

"I'm glad I was one of the Groupies that waved you off at Biarritz," said Bridget. "We might have hired a car and joined in these civic receptions."

"This is only make believe you know Bridget," said Ray her husband.

"Don't be so tiresome, you boring old fart! Let's see where imagination might lead," Jeff rollicked him.

"The crowds would have grown bigger as we cycled north and as more and more people logged into the web site, keen to get in the photo-shoot," Paul continued.

"That's when we would start to find French people wearing GASBAGS shirts," I said.

"That's a bit far fetched," responded John.

"Not really," I said. "I told Tony Orrell of Torellisport, who made our shirts, about this ride. He would have heard about the ride in the national press and seen the opportunity coming to sell lots of shirts. He would have diverted the Belgium factory to producing just GASBAGS shirts."

"A good job Jeff was not on the ride. He would probably have changed the route at the last moment, as he is renowned for doing, leaving crowds of GASBAGS supporters with no-one to support," Pam said giggling.

"The mayors would have upgraded our accommodation and provided us with feasts and massages thrown in. I fancy a massage off a nubile young French woman," Paul said with his eyes shining either with the thoughts of the women or the four pints he had consumed.

"My website, sorry our website, would start to get lots of hits as our ride became national news both in the UK and France," I said with my eyes gleaming.

"Naoko would ensure that the Japanese knew about the ride and thousands of hits would come from the far-east," Zoe remarked, now on her fourth pint of cider, her favourite tipple, and able to drink most men under the table.

"I got one email from Australia," I said, "My friend there said 'You realize you might have started something with all that inspirational commentary'. So we would get all of Australia onboard the website easily."

"By this time Tony Orrell would be having difficulty with keeping up with the GASBAGS shirts demand as orders flooded in from England, France, Japan and Australia," Paul laughed.

"You're all as stupid as each other," John said.

"We would be invited to meet the French president," said Paul excitedly.

"Well I wouldn't go," said Ray.

"Nor me," said John.

"It's only fantasy you know," I said. "Perhaps year 2005 would become the first year that the Tour de France bike ride served beer to the riders at their refreshment stops in recognition of our achievement."

"We could get the GASBAGS songwriter to write a theme song for us called 'God save the GASBAGS'," Pam exclaimed. "Let's all sing the song he wrote, 'We all ride on a GASBAG Mountain Bike' sung to the Yellow Submarine music. I will lead."

At which point everyone cleared their throats and sang loudly:

> "In the town where I was born, lived a man
> Whose name was Mike
> And he told us of his life
> In the land of Mountain bikes
> So we rode off to the sun, till we found a pub
> We liked
> And we stopped off for a beer
> On a GASBAGS's Mountain bike
> We all ride on a GASBAG Mountain Bike
> And our friends have joined the club
> Plenty more of them are in the pub
> And the girls have joined as well
> Now the GASBAGS rides are just like heaven
> We all…"

The rest of the pub were staring into their drinks by the end wishing we would go away.

"Perhaps other biking and guzzling societies will start to spring up," I said. "We would need a constitution that would state that all affiliated club names must end in 'BAGS'."

"There could be some good titles like SAPBAGS for Southampton and Portsmouth, and FABBAGS for Flint and Buckley," Jeff came in quickly.

"I'm president," Bushy Ray said. "The constitution must state that all affiliated clubs should be called 'GASBAGS' as the dictionary definition of gasbagging is 'people who chatter too much', and that's us."

"How about us all cycling across America next year," Zoe remarked. "Then we would all become famous."

"You're fanaticising again," John rebuked.

"I fancy that," said Paul. "We could sell GASBAGS bike shirts with our photographs and names on the back like football shirts."

"You could just use a photograph of a bald headed man with a beard for you men as it would be cheaper. Most of you have lost your hair—except for my Craig," Zoe said stroking her husband's hair.

"I've not got a beard nor am I bald," I said pulling my hair hard trying to make it reach my eyebrows.

"I can see it," said Jeff. "Many of the younger men would buy shirts with 'Zoe' on the back."

"The young women would want 'Craig' on the shirt," said Bridget. "I would buy one even though I have just turned fifty. I fancy his animal magnetism."

"Hey. This could lead to the public becoming bored with Posh and Becks and switching their attention to Zoe and Craig," I said.

"Finally we could end up at Hollywood like the Calendar girls," Paul exclaimed.

"I think it's time to go home before we start to believe in this fantasy," Ray remarked then stood up and walked out.

## Sponsorship

By the time we returned the sponsorship total on the website had reached just over £2,800 but Paul was expecting more to come through from his solicitor contacts. I still hoped that John would finally raise some sponsorship and fulfil his commitment.

Paul had set up an account in his Building Society called "Paul Greenhalgh—Cycling Challenge" and we all agreed that we would pay the sponsorship we raised into this account.

I set to at Dupont-Teijin Films collecting the money I had raised there. A few students had sponsored me but by the time I returned they had returned to University so I missed out. A few people who had sponsored me had also been involved in sponsored events so I felt obliged to give the same—asking for sponsorship can become expensive! When we had started to collect sponsorship I had quickly approached all the GAS-BAGS members to swell my total so it was unfair upon Paul and Ray. I finally raised just over £1,100.

Ray sent a cheque for about £300 to Paul, and then lo and behold John sent a cheque to Paul for about £300. John had actually raised sponsorship but never entered his sponsorship on the website as Paul and I had continually asked him to. At least he had tried.

Paul was quite confident that he would be able to swell his total so that the combined total would go past £3,000.

## Publicity

Paul and I were still keen after arriving home to see if we could get more sponsorship from the wider Teesside population. We hoped that the actual completion of the ride and the achievement of four over-fifties having ridden 900 miles would prompt extra sponsorship.

Paul contacted Stuart McFarlane at Radio Cleveland and arranged that he and I would again be on Stuart's radio show. The Radio Cleveland bus was being taken to Stokesley Show on Saturday September 18th and Stuart asked us to turn up there. Stokesley Show is an annual event and besides being an agricultural show showing the best bulls, cows, sheep etc there were also horse jumping events, pets on show, and many outdoors clothes shops. The event attracts a wide audience and I imagined that Stuart's voice would be broadcast across the fields, with a good chance of our acquaintances hearing our plea for more sponsorship. We turned up and were interviewed with Paul now having his patter about raising money for charities even more finely tuned. I managed to get in a few words about the challenge and my parents having Alzheimer's. Unfortunately though the broadcast was just to the fifty or so Radio Cleveland listeners and not to those at the show—an opportunity lost.

I wrote a review of the ride with a plea for more sponsorship and sent it off to the Stream, the Teesside Gazette, the Darlington and Stockton Times and Bob Lappin, our publicity agent. Bob contacted me and rewrote parts of the article and entitled it, 'They biked, guzzled and made it' with the article appearing in the Darlington & Stockton Times. The article forgot to include the website address but did include the words "Anyone who would like to sponsor their chosen good causes should contact Mike Newton or Paul Greenhalgh" and our phone numbers were given.

I received an email from Carol Morgan, the editor of the Stream magazine:

"Hi, Mike. I was going to contact you soon to see if you wanted to amend your original item, as you said you might, but then I saw the photo & article in the D & S.

I'm delighted for you that you were given such well-earned publicity with such a wide catchment area, but I was dismayed to see that the article was almost word for word the same as you had sent to me for the not-yet-printed Stream….it will look as if I have simply taken it straight from the D&S & printed it without acknowledgement, which I would never do. Apart from the unprofessionalism of doing that, I try to avoid repeating things that have already been printed, for the sake of the readership—I don't want people to stop reading it because they think they will already have read much of it elsewhere. Could you re-work your piece, please, introducing some new details?"

That evening I re-wrote the article to be more about the planning of the ride and the good causes and sent it off—I did not intend to miss the opportunity for more publicity. The next day I received another email from Carol:

"Very Dear Mike—bless you! The new version is exactly the right sort of thing (though, if I dare say it, rather longer than I have room for—I shall have to "squeeze" it somewhat!)

Thank you so much for responding so quickly—it gives me time to do it justice"

I had never met Carol but her writing comes across as very bubbly and effusive. I thought what a jolly person—I wondered if she had played hockey when she was younger?
She wrote later that the article was too long and that she would reduce it to fit onto one page or one and a half pages if she could squeeze other articles. I sent a reply saying could she keep in what I thought was my most amusing line "Mike almost took Contac 400 instead of diarrhoea tablets which would have been fine for a runny nose but not a runny bottom" but she replied saying it would have to be left out as the article

was too long. Perhaps she did not like my warped sense of humour.

I waited with bated breath for the article to appear and Carol had been able to give us one and a half pages with the article entitled "The GASBAGS Tour through Twinned Towns—Before and after". On the page before the Great Ayton Twinning association (GATA) had just a half page article. I could not help smiling to myself that we had more space after the rumour that GATA may have intervened to stop our Ouzouer mayoral contact. The article again gave our contact details for anyone who would like to sponsor us.

After all this publicity we were hoping that more sponsorship would come through but I have to admit that no-one phoned either myself or Paul to offer sponsorship nor did anyone unknown add sponsorship on the website.

### The following weeks

Paul still had his goal of riding 10,000 miles in the year and continued to go on rides whenever he had a spare moment. However his work picked up and he realised he would need to reduce his goal to beating his achievement of 9,300 miles at the age of nineteen. I joined him on a few nine and twenty mile rides at 7:00 am when it was still dark as we set off and also very cold. He finally cycled his new target of 9,500 miles just before the New Year.

Paul also took his wife Liz for a long weekend to Biarritz for a surprise fiftieth birthday holiday. He sent me an email when he returned:

"Beach was still great—not so many holiday swimmers, but the local surfers were out in force. Temps are still 75 to 80 degs. Did not see Murielle this time, but Julia of RyanAir was doing our return flight to Stansted. Liz accepted why I had gone on about her, but pointed out to me during the flight that

I did not need to dribble every time I looked in Julia's direction. Can confirm again that Julia does not have a squint."

Paul began to be absent from the weekly Sunday bike rides and our Thursday night social nights. I sent him a note asking if he had to pay "retribution" which he did not understand—I had meant to say "penance". In fact his work was taking him all over the country. Liz said a loud "no" to being his backup the following August if he cycled the Pyrenees, so he aims to have two weeks away in October 2005.

Ray gave up his idea of cycling across Iceland and thinks he will hire a jeep if he does go. He met a new girlfriend, shortly after he returned, who cycles and he has given her a training regime to get fit for next year's GASBAGS mixed ride.

John has only been seen once since the ride. We did learn that John is remarkably fit and likes challenges so I would expect to hear about him going on an exotic challenge soon once he retires from Corus.

I had entered myself in the Great North Run at the start of the year. I had never been in the run before but several of the GASBAGS members had taken part the year before and intended to put their names down. However only I and one other GASBAG were accepted with the rest missing the deadline. I was unsure whether I would be able to partake as I had suffered from Achilles tendonitis for over two years. I knew that I could not afford to practice very much or my Achilles would flare up. I was not a fast runner; in fact I was very slow. I had taken part several times in the annual New Years Day five-mile run from the Great Ayton Royal Oak pub up to the Captain monument and back. I normally came close to being last and one year just beat a sixty-year old who walked round with a stick. However I had running the Great North Run as a life goal. After returning from France I ran four short practice runs then on September 24th I ran in the Great North

Run. I ran all the way except for a 5 minute toilet break, and achieved a time of 2 hours 30 minutes when running. I later received a certificate saying that I had come 32,456 out of a field of 39,000, which I found strange when 49,000 took part. Are there still 10,000 running round? There is no doubt in my mind that the 914-mile cycle ride built up my stamina and helped my running.

Paul had been receiving a few donations over the months since the ride. We finally decided to totalise the donations just before Christmas. I proposed that we should send each charity a Christmas card signed by each of us. However it was after Christmas by the time Paul had time to work out the totals and on Boxing Day the Tsunami struck in the Indian Ocean with over 220,000 deaths. One group of solicitors who were going to donate £200 to MacMillan Cancer Care Nursing decided to send their money straight to Medecins sans Frontieres but the money had been raised at Paul's request so we felt it fair to include in our total.

The total for each charity worked out as:

| | |
|---|---|
| MacMillan Cancer Care Nursing | £1401 |
| The Alzheimer's Society | £720 |
| The National Asthma Campaign | £570 |
| Yatton House | £466 |
| Medecins sans Frontieres | £250 |
| Total | £3407 |

Paul sent the cheques off to the local branches of the Alzheimer's Society and the MacMillan cancer relief charity, to the central organisation for the National Asthma Campaign, and to Yatton House. Within a few days he had thank you letters from all the organisations.

The letter from Barbara Starmer of the Alzheimer's Society was particularly effervescent:

"Dear Paul…What a superb way to raise money. Thanks also for the lovely card. I will ensure that all of this money is used to help people with dementia, their families and carers in the Teesside area…Donations such as yours are extremely valuable in enabling us to continue that work…"

The letter from Stephanie Wood of MacMillan cancer relief was very kind:

"Dear Paul…thank you…in respect of your recent 914 mile bike ride through France—undertaken with Mike, Ray and John, all of whom are absolute stars. It is wonderful when donations such as this come into the office and it is a real boost for February's funds. It is also an amazing amount and for this we are extremely grateful.

This donation will enable us to fund further Macmillan nurses, GPs and other healthcare specialists, give out Macmillan grants to people who are in financial difficulties because of their illness and build cancer care centres where expert treatment, care and information is available for anyone who needs it…."

The letter from J Lindo of Yatton House was much briefer (but just as sincere as I know the ex-manager and how important it is to receive donations):

"Dear Paul…thank you for the donation…raised through sponsorship for your marathon bike ride across France.

Please be assured that the money will be put to very good use in a practical way…"

The letter from Gary McGinn from Asthma UK showed the importance of raising money for asthma research:

"Dear Paul, Mike, Ray & John…Your France bike ride last August and September sounds like it was an amazing adventure. We are delighted you completed the tour successfully and hopefully without incident. Can you please pass on our thanks to all your sponsors who asked to support Asthma UK.

One in six people with severe asthma symptoms report weekly attacks so severe they cannot speak—5.2 million people in the UK have asthma. Asthma is a major concern in our community and Asthma UK is the only charity dedicated to the health and well being of people with asthma. We fund an asthma research programme which costs £3 million every year to run and on a practical front our Asthma Advise Line offers confidential and independent advice from asthma nurse specialists…"

These letters made the time spent gaining sponsorship prior to the ride and collecting it in after the ride seem all worthwhile.

# Endpiece

Paul and I had started out with the objective of cycling across France and raising as much money as we could for charity. We had completed the ride successfully. There had been no punctures at all and the only bike repair required had been the replacement of John's bikes bottom bracket. The team spirit had been excellent, and except for the odd small argument, we had all got on well. The team had stopped to await the slower cyclists at the right intervals, and we had only gone the wrong way once,

Each evening we had eaten together and no one had done their own thing—almost remarkable over a three-week period. I did wonder afterwards what it would have been like if I had gone by myself or if just Paul and I had gone. Josie Dew cycles all over the world mainly by herself and really enjoys cycling by herself as she finds it much easier to meet people along the way, but Josie is an attractive slim woman. Possibly Paul and I would have spent more time getting to know about the places that we stopped at.

We raised over £3,400 for charity and we were pleased with that amount but I had set an unrealistic goal of £10,000. I believe the website had been a great success in keeping those that were interested informed of our progress, and it did act as a central point to totalise the sponsorship, However the personal entry of sponsorship directly onto the website had been a failure. Very few people were prepared to give sponsorship unless they were personally approached and a piece of paper stuck under their nose to add their sponsorship. Obtaining sponsorship from the French and Japanese through the website had been a total failure. We will never know how many people read, either in English or French, the write-ups about the French and English twinned towns. Our letters to the French mayors had largely been ignored and we did not even meet the mayor of Ouzouer.

However Paul and I enjoyed planning the ride and thinking of ways to get sponsorship. We were advised that we should have started the planning a year earlier to allow for more possibility of raising greater sponsorship.

I personally felt that the ride was a great achievement, and very happy that my weight had reduced from 16 st 8 lbs to 15 st 10 lb, as my Japanese partner had kept telling me to lose weight.

The reception we had received from all the French people that we met was outstanding and they all had a great generosity of spirit. I wondered if the European Union is bringing the reward of integration and togetherness. I remember feeling a strange moment of pride and euphoria on May 1st, the day when an additional ten countries joined the EU viz Cyprus, the Czech Republic, Estonia, Hungary, Latvia, Lithuania, Malta, Poland, Slovakia and Slovenia. We in the UK could now go to twenty-four other countries and have that feeling that we have common values and aims. I felt that the UK was now part of a large club that could start to compete with the USA for being leader of the Western world, and perhaps more importantly we could sit at the same table as the USA, India and China as these latter two, with their enormous populations, rapidly increase in prosperity. But do we have the politicians that will grasp this opportunity and not defend the 'Little Britain' backward reality? I only hope so as many of the people who elected President Bush believe in Christian religious fundamentalism, and are now even questioning the Darwin theory of evolution.

Perhaps the follow-on from this ride could be 'The Tour through the European Union' cycling through every capital of the twenty-five countries, with team members taken from all of the countries. The aim could be to meet each country's head of state. The ride could capture the imagination of the combined population of 450 million, and aid in the ratification of the European constitution and the adoption of the Euro. Perhaps just a dream…

# Appendix

## Appendix A  Luggage and Equipment

Clothes
- Bike shirts, bike shorts, socks, underpants, shirts, headbands, handkerchiefs (3 of each)
- Trunks—just in case we had the chance to swim and we did in Biarritz
- Shoes—bike shoes and sandals
- Hat
- Long trousers—I was concerned about mosquitoes and assumed that we would need to cover up in the evening—I took tracksuit bottoms. Ray took rather smart white trousers so I assumed that he would be on the lookout for women
- Warm top—I took my tracksuit top
- Cycling gloves—I was the only one to take gloves and only wore them once
- Raincoat—Karrimor Gore-tex Paclite

Health
- Lifeventure Micro-fibre Giant and small trek towels
- Toothpaste & brush
- Shaving cream & razor
- Flannel
- Soap
- Soap powder
- Insect repellent
- Sun block

- Lip salve with sun block—which I never used
- Canestan cream—which I never used
- Medicines
- Imodium
- 10 x GO Energy bars (Cherry & Vanilla, Chocolate & Orange")
- GO Electrolyte powder
- 6 x GO GEL with isotonic energy sachets (Orange, Blackcurrant, Tropical)
- Toilet roll
- Nail cutters
- Wet-ones

Miscellaneous
- Passport
- E111 form
- Insurance documents
- Driving License
- Photocopies—Passport, cards
- Address List etc
- Notebook
- Nikon Coolpix 2200 Digital Camera
- Sony HandyCam DCR-HC30E Camcorder (very small and weighing less than one pound)
- French Sponsorship Business Cards
- Maps
- French books
- Hotel directions
- Hotel bookings
- Flight bookings
- Currency
- Laptop
- Mobile phone
- Bike lock
- Spare glasses

- Sunglasses
- French plug adapter
- Corkscrew

Bike panniers
- Altura Orkney 50 litre rear panniers
- Altura Orkney 8 litre Bar Bag
- Altura Arran 8 litre rack pack

Bike spares
- Chain
- Chain remover
- Inner tubes
- Tyre repair kit
- Spanners
- Screw drivers
- Water bottles
- Tyre levers
- Chain lube & a rag
- Allen keys
- Phillips screwdriver
- Small flat screwdriver
- Spare brake pads
- Spare screws and bolts for rack etc
- Spoke key
- Spare spokes and nipples
- Pliers
- Spare chain links
- Gear cables
- Tape
- Nylon ties

# Appendix B  Sponsorship

### MacMillan Cancer Care Nursing
www.macmillan.org.uk

Macmillan Cancer Relief is a UK charity that works to improve the quality of life for people living with cancer. Currently over a million people are living with cancer in the UK and, if current trends continue, more than five million will be diagnosed between now and 2020.

Macmillan offers life support by providing the expert care and practical support that makes a difference to people living with cancer.

### The Alzheimer's Society
www.alzheimers.org.uk

The Alzheimer's Society is committed to maintaining, improving and promoting its unique knowledge and understanding of dementia.

It seeks to define and develop quality in its care and core services, to reach out to and include all people with dementia, their families and the professionals who work with them and to work in partnership with other organisations that share its aims.

### The National Asthma Campaign
www.asthma.org.uk/

The National Asthma Campaign is the independent UK charity dedicated to conquering asthma. It funds asthma research, offers help and advice and campaigns for a better deal for people with asthma.

Paula Radcliffe MBE says, "5.1 million people have asthma in the UK, including 1 in 8 children. Having asthma myself I understand the importance of the work of the National Asthma Campaign. This is why I have agreed to captain their 2004 Flora London Marathon runners' team. Help us to help more people take control of their asthma. And join us to raise £455,000 for vital asthma research."

## Yatton House
www.northallertonmencap.org.uk/wayahead_dayservices.htm

This is run by a voluntary organisation affiliated to MENCAP. Their philosophy is to encourage and enable their members to achieve their full potential and to give everyone as much opportunity as possible for integration into the community.

Each member has an individual life plan, which shows their strengths, as well as a short and long-term plan to build on these with appropriate skills.

Activities are varied and include integrated leisure, drama therapy, numeracy, literacy, and independent living skills. Some members attend a college of further education, evening classes and others have work experience placements.

## Medecins sans Frontieres
www.msf.com

Medecins Sans Frontieres is an independent humanitarian medical aid agency, which is committed to two objectives:
- Providing medical aid wherever it is needed, regardless of race, religion, politics or sex.
- Raising awareness of the plight of the people we help.

Medecins Sans Frontieres was founded in 1971, in the wake of the war of the Biafra and the floods in Pakistan. Today, the association has become one of the main humanitarian organizations that provides medical help.

MSF brings medical aid to the populations in crisis, when their health or their survival is threatened. They may be victims of violence, war, famine, epidemics, natural disasters, or displacement. These crises require the fast and efficient interventions to assist the local structures, to take care of the injured and sick, and to re-establish the conditions of decent life, while assuring provision in water, nutrition, purification, and the construction of shelters.

# Appendix C  Hotels

| Date | | Accommodation | |
|---|---|---|---|
| 18-Aug | Biarritz | Tulip Inn | £24 |
| 20-Aug | St Palais | Hotel du Midi | £20 |
| 21-Aug | Pau | Hotel du Commerce (Logis de France) | £22 |
| 22-Aug | Auch | Hotel Campanile | £19* |
| 23-Aug | Agen | Hotel Le Perigord (Logis de France) | £25 |
| 24-Aug | Belves | Hotel Belvedere de Belves (breakfast extra) | £18 |
| 25-Aug | Collonges | La Vigne Grande (Chambre D'Hote) | £15 |
| 26-Aug | Treignac | Maury (Gites de France) | £14 |
| 27-Aug | Benevent L'Abbaye | La Buissonniere (Chambre D'Hote) | £15 |
| 28-Aug | Argenton-sur-Creuse | Hotel L'Esplanade (Logis de France) | £18 |
| 30-Aug | Aubigny | Auberge La Fontaine (Logis de France) | £22 |
| 02-Sep | Bonneval | Hotel de France (Logis de France) | £29** |
| 03-Sep | Belleme | Hotel Le Relais St Louis (Logis de France) | £29** |
| 04-Sep | Falaise | Hotel La Poste (Logis de France) | £24 |

\*   breakfast extra
\*\*  evening meal included

# Appendix D  Sponsorship Messages

Most of the entries on the website had been entered by Paul and myself from filled-in forms which we had used to embarrass people into sponsoring us. However quite a few had entered their sponsorship directly on the website leaving messages of support:

- Well done. I've been asthmatic all my life so it's a charity dear to my heart, especially these days when it seems to be more prevalent.
- Donated in memory of my mother who was a life-long asthma sufferer.
- My mother has Alzheimer's so I have seen at first hand how people can be transformed.
- Donated in memory of my dad who was given great support by the wonderful MacMillan nurses.
- We have selected this charity as we have experienced the great work Macmillan's do in helping people cope with cancer.
- Towards my keep as I'm sure I will end up there—Alzheimer's Society.
- You should let your youth slip away gracefully you old buggers………good luck!!!!
- Came for a meal at Paul & Liz's and gone home £50 lighter!
- Payable upon you both completing every mile on a bike. (That is a hint to do more training Mike!)
- I always thought my brother Ray was mad! He's got more energy than me but a nuttier streak!

- Sorry we are late…just wanted to be sure you would finish. Knowing John, could there ever have been a doubt well done all of you
- I hope that you are laying off the Boddies Paul during your preparation, even though it was part of your staple diet while you lived in Manchester.
- Fit a soft saddle or wear the padded pants!
- Helping Paul with applying his vaseline during the training period—anyone else in need of help?
- Hi Mike, Paul Mack from Stokesley ride, hope all has gone well for you all and all are safe and well. France and the French people are fabulous towards cyclists
- I hope that you all have a good trip and that you have not had to resort to a cocktail of illegal drugs as most serious cyclists seem to these days!
- I'm surprised you didn't consider the British Haemorrhoids Society to be worthy of sponsorship!— You will by the end of the trip!!

# Appendix E   Possible Tour through the EU

| Country | Capital | Population | Bike Part Mileage | Ferry |
|---|---|---|---|---|
| Portugal | Lisbon | 9.9 | Fly | |
| Spain | Madrid | 39.6 | 397 | |
| Italy | Rome | 57.3 | 376 | Yes |
| Malta | Valletta | 0.4 | 136 | Yes |
| Greece | Athens | 10.6 | 241 | Yes |
| Cyprus | Nicosia | 0.8 | 10 | Yes |
| Slovenia | Ljubljana | 2 | 140 | Yes |
| Hungary | Budapest | 10 | 303 | |
| Slovakia | Bratislava | 5.4 | 127 | |
| Austria | Vienna | 8.2 | 40 | |
| Czech | Prague | 10.2 | 178 | |
| Germany | Berlin | 82.2 | 230 | |
| Poland | Warsaw | 38.8 | 354 | |
| Lithuania | Vilnius | 3.7 | 347 | |
| Latvia | Riga | 2.4 | 191 | |
| Estonia | Tallinn | 1.4 | 198 | |
| Finland | Helsinki | 5.2 | 10 | Yes |
| Sweden | Stockholm | 8.9 | 10 | Yes |
| Denmark | Copenhagen | 5.3 | 382 | |
| Netherlands | Amsterdam | 15.8 | 465 | |
| Belgium | Brussels | 10.2 | 156 | |
| Luxembourg | Luxembourg | 0.4 | 132 | |
| France | Paris | 59.1 | 203 | |
| UK | London | 58.8 | 267 | Yes |
| Ireland | Dublin | 3.7 | 265 | Yes |
| **Total** | | | **5158** | |

# Appendix F   The Diary & Photographs

I had the opportunity to test out the updating of a website whilst on the move in March 2004 when I spent a month in Japan. I built a website showing a diagram of Japan and the locations I would visit, and I downloaded the website to the free web space that is provided if you have a Freeserve account. I then created one page on the website to download the diary and photographs.

When I arrived in Japan I tested out the website updating but found it would not work as I could not log directly into Freeserve. I sent a note to a friend who I knew had built a Freeserve-based website and he agreed to update the site for me if I sent him the diary and photographs by email on a daily basis. I toured round Okinawa, Kyoto, and Izumo and sent through the diary and photographs from the PC's installed in the hotels. The website was read by many of my friends and work colleagues. I knew now that it would be possible to transmit a daily diary from France.

I learnt that it would not be possible to login to Freeserve on an '0845' number when in France. I contacted Wanadoo, the French company that owns Freeserve, hoping that they could provide me with a French phone number for me to access my Freeserve account, as besides wanting to update the website, I also wanted to exchange emails with Naoko. They said it was not possible but hoped to provide this facility some time in the future which was not much good to me. Freeserve is a fairly recent Wanadoo acquisition and I got the impression that little interaction had yet taken place between the two companies. I checked with Wanadoo to see if I could open a Wanadoo Internet account but they said only if I had a French fixed-line phone number that I did not have. I began to feel snookered but then searched on the Internet for any company that provided local phone number logins to access the Internet in different countries, and found one called 'Net2Roam'. Their service cost £55 to join and then calls would cost 12 pence/minute plus the local phone charges. I explained all the above to Paul and he was prepared to fund half of the costs.

I assumed that most of the cheap Hotels we had chosen would not have phone lines to the rooms. I thought I would go through my mobile phone and use a Bluetooth PCMCIA card in my PC to transmit to the mobile. However if I went through my mobile the link to the local French number would still go back to the UK and be charged at 60 pence a minute, so I decided I would buy a 'Pay as you go' SIMM card in France to go in my mobile. I had my mobile unlocked for £15 (allowing any SIMM card to go in it).

However when I arrived in France that it was not possible to transmit data with a 'Pay as you go' SIMM card and I was not prepared to fund a contract mobile phone.

Fortunately it turned out that most hotels did provide access to a phone line that could link through to the Internet, and the purchase of a French phone connector provided me with a fixed link.

978-0-595-41760-5
0-595-41760-4

Printed in Great Britain
by Amazon.co.uk, Ltd.,
Marston Gate.